Yamaha
Passola
Owners
Workshop
Manual

by Pete Shoemark

Models covered
SA50 M Passola. 49cc. Introduced May 1980
SA50 ME Passola. 49cc. Introduced July 1982

ISBN 1 85010 155 8

ABCDE
FGHIJ
KLMNO
PQ

Printed in England   *(733-5K1)*

Haynes Publishing Group
Sparkford Nr Yeovil
Somerset BA22 7JJ England

Haynes Publications, Inc
861 Lawrence Drive
Newbury Park
California 91320 USA

British Library Cataloguing in Publication Data
Shoemark, Pete
Yamaha SA50 Passola owners workshop manual.–
2nd ed.– (Haynes owners workshop manuals)
1. Passola moped
I. Title   II. Shoemark, Pete. Yamaha Passola
owners workshop manual   III. Series
629.28'772   TL443
ISBN 1–85010–155–8

Acknowledgements

Our thanks are due to Jim Patch of Yeovil Motorcycle Services who loaned the Yamaha Passola featured in this manual. Mitsui Machinery Sales (UK) Ltd provided valuable technical data and gave permission to reproduce many of the line drawings.

NGK Spark Plugs (UK) Ltd supplied information on sparking plug maintenance and electrode condition and the Avon Rubber Company assisted with information and advice on tyre fitting.

About this manual

The purpose of this manual is to present the owner with a concise and graphic guide which will enable him to tackle any operation from basic routine maintenance to a major overhaul. It has been assumed that any work would be undertaken without the luxury of a well-equipped workshop and a range of manufacturer's service tools.

To this end, the machine featured in the manual was stripped and rebuilt in our own workshop, by a team comprising a mechanic, a photographer and the author. The resulting photographic sequence depicts events as they took place, the hands shown being those of the author and the mechanic.

The use of specialised, and expensive, service tools was avoided unless their use was considered to be essential due to risk of breakage or injury. There is usually some way of improvising a method of removing a stubborn component, provided that a suitable degree of care is exercised.

The author learnt his motorcycle mechanics over a number of years, faced with the same difficulties and using similar facilities to those encountered by most owners. It is hoped that this practical experience can be passed on through the pages of this manual.

Where possible, a well-used example of the machine is chosen for the workshop project, as this highlights any areas which might be particularly prone to giving rise to problems. In this way, any such difficulties are encountered and resolved before the text is written, and the techniques used to deal with them can be incorporated in the relevant sections. Armed with a working knowledge of the machine, the author undertakes a considerable amount of reseach in order that the maximum amount of data can be included in this manual.

Each Chapter is divided into numbered sections. Within these sections are numbered paragraphs. Cross reference throughout the manual is quite straightforward and logical. When reference is made 'See Section 6.10' it means Section 6, paragraph 10 in the same Chapter. If another Chapter were intended the reference would read, for example, 'See Chapter 2, Section 6.10'. All the photographs are captioned with a section/paragraph number to which they refer and are relevant to the Chapter text adjacent.

Figures (usually line illustrations) appear in a logical but numerical order, within a given Chapter. Fig. 1.1 therefore refers to the first figure in Chapter 1.

Left-hand and right-hand descriptions of the machines and their components refer to the left and right of a given machine when the rider is seated normally.

Motorcycle manufacturers continually make changes to specifications and recommendations, and these, when notified, are incorporated into our manuals at the earliest opportunity.

Whilst every care is taken to ensure that the information in this manual is correct no liability can be accepted by the author or publishers for loss, damage or injury caused by any errors in or omissions from the information given.

Contents

Left-hand view of the 1981 Yamaha Passola

Right-hand view of the 1981 Yamaha Passola

Engine and transmission unit of the 1981 Yamaha Passola

Introduction to the Yamaha Passola

The Passola represents one of the first serious attempts by a major motorcycle manufacturer to exploit a previously untapped market. The recent dramatic increases in world oil prices have made many car and public transport users think seriously about alternative methods of getting to and from work. In addition there are many women who would not consider a powered two-wheeler as a practical means of transport, being wary of the motorcycle's masculine and oily image.

To attract these potential buyers, Yamaha have chosen to opt for an extremely economical fully automatic moped, with nearly all of the mechanical components hidden behind body panels. The result is a blend of Japanese technology and Italian scooter styling and layout. The number of controls has been kept to a minimum, often at the expense of astonishing complexity beneath the body panels, a good example being a sophisticated vacuum fuel tap and choke, both of which are fully automatic in operation and have no manual controls, but which relay instead on a complex network of tubes and valves.

The major handlebar controls are limited to two brake levers and a throttle control. The fully automatic transmission means that riding the Passola is as simple as it could be, and is simplified to the stage where the rider needs only to open the throttle to accelerate and to apply the brakes to stop.

The UK version has a two-speed transmission which is governed by road and engine speeds, being fully automatic in operation. This provides brisk acceleration up to about 30 mph; the prescribed maximum speed for mopeds. The version supplied to certain Europeans has a single speed transmission but has a similar performance overall.

At the time of writing, the Passola is proving very popular in its intended market, and has induced the production of a similar machine from at least one rival factory.

Model dimensions and weight

Length	1580 mm (62.2 in)
Width	615 mm (24.2 in)
Height	940 mm (37.0 in)
Seat height	715 mm (28.1 in)
Ground clearance	110 mm (4.3 in)
Wheelbase	1115 mm (43.9 in)
Dry weight	51 kg (112 lb)

Ordering spare parts

When replacement parts are required for your Passola it is advisable to deal direct with a recognised Yamaha agent or with the area distributor. They are better placed to supply the parts ex-stock and should have the technical experience that may not be available with other suppliers. When ordering spare parts, always quote the engine and frame numbers in full, since these will identify the model and its date of manufacture. It will sometimes help if the old part is presented when the replacement is ordered, to aid correct identification.

Always refit replacement parts of Yamaha manufacture and do not be tempted to use pattern parts. Although the pattern parts may appear similar they often give inferior service and may prove more expensive in the long run. In addition the use of parts not supplied by Yamaha may invalidate subsequent warranty claims.

The engine number is stamped on the rear of the transmission casing, adjacent to the rear brake. The frame number is stamped on the right-hand side of the steering head.

Some of the more expendable parts such as sparking plugs, bulbs, tyres, oils and greases etc also can be obtained from accessory shops and motor factors, who have convenient opening hours, and can often be found not far from home. It is also possible to obtain parts on a Mail Order basis from a number of specialists who advertise regularly in the motorcycle magazines.

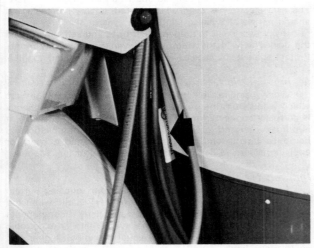

Location of frame number

Location of engine number

Safety First!

Professional motor mechanics are trained in safe working procedures. However enthusiastic you may be about getting on with the job in hand, do take the time to ensure that your safety is not put at risk. A moment's lack of attention can result in an accident, as can failure to observe certain elementary precautions.

There will always be new ways of having accidents, and the following points do not pretend to be a comprehensive list of all dangers; they are intended rather to make you aware of the risks and to encourage a safety-conscious approach to all work you carry out on your vehicle.

Essential DOs and DON'Ts

DON'T start the engine without first ascertaining that the machine is on its centre stand.

DON'T attempt to drain oil until you are sure it has cooled sufficiently to avoid scalding you.

DON'T grasp any part of the engine, exhaust or silencer without first ascertaining that it is sufficiently cool to avoid burning you.

DON'T syphon toxic liquids such as fuel, brake fluid or antifreeze by mouth, or allow them to remain on your skin.

DON'T inhale brake lining dust — it is injurious to health.

DON'T allow any spilt oil or grease to remain on the floor — wipe it up straight away, before someone slips on it.

DON'T use ill-fitting spanners or other tools which may slip and cause injury.

DON'T attempt to lift a heavy component which may be beyond your capability — get assistance.

DON'T rush to finish a job, or take unverified short cuts.

DON'T allow children or animals in or around an unattended vehicle.

DON'T inflate a tyre to a pressure above the recommended maximum. Apart from overstressing the carcase and wheel rim, in extreme cases the tyre may blow off forcibly.

DO ensure that the machine is supported securely at all times. This is especially important when the machine is blocked up to aid wheel or fork removal.

DO take care when attempting to slacken a stubborn nut or bolt. It is generally better to pull on a spanner, rather than push, so that if slippage occurs you fall away from the machine rather than on to it.

DO wear eye protection when using power tools such as drill, sander, bench grinder etc.

DO use a barrier cream on your hands prior to undertaking dirty jobs — it will protect your skin from infection as well as making the dirt easier to remove afterwards; but make sure your hands aren't left slippery.

DO keep loose clothing (cuffs, tie etc) and long hair well out of the way of moving mechanical parts.

DO remove rings, wristwatch etc, before working on the vehicle — especially the electrical system.

DO keep your work area tidy — it is only too easy to fall over articles left lying around.

DO exercise caution when compressing springs for removal or installation. Ensure that the tension is applied and released in a controlled manner, using suitable tools which preclude the possibility of the spring escaping violently.

DO ensure that any lifting tackle used has a safe working load rating adequate for the job.

DO get someone to check periodically that all is well, when working alone on the vehicle.

DO carry out work in a logical sequence and check that everything is correctly assembled and tightened afterwards.

DO remember that your vehicle's safety affects that of yourself and others. If in doubt on any point, get specialist advice.

IF, in spite of following these precautions, you are unfortunate enough to injure yourself, seek medical attention as soon as possible.

Fire

Remember at all times that petrol (gasoline) is highly flammable. Never smoke, or have any kind of naked flame around, when working on the vehicle. But the risk does not end there — a spark caused by an electrical short-circuit, by two metal surfaces contacting each other, or even by static electricity built up in your body under certain conditions, can ignite petrol vapour, which in a confined space is highly explosive.

Always disconnect the battery earth (ground) terminal before working on any part of the fuel system, and never risk spilling fuel on to a hot engine or exhaust.

It is recommended that a fire extinguisher of a type suitable for fuel and electrical fires is kept handy in the garage or workplace at all times. Never try to extinguish a fuel or electrical fire with water.

Fumes

Certain fumes are highly toxic and can quickly cause unconsciousness and even death if inhaled to any extent. Petrol (gasoline) vapour comes into this category, as do the vapours from certain solvents such as trichloroethylene. Any draining or pouring of such volatile fluids should be done in a well ventilated area.

When using cleaning fluids and solvents, read the instructions carefully. Never use materials from unmarked containers — they may give off poisonous vapours.

Never run the engine of a motor vehicle in an enclosed space such as a garage. Exhaust fumes contain carbon monoxide which is extremely poisonous; if you need to run the engine, always do so in the open air or at least have the rear of the vehicle outside the workplace.

If you are fortunate enough to have the use of an inspection pit, never drain or pour petrol, and never run the engine, while the vehicle is standing over it; the fumes, being heavier than air, will concentrate in the pit with possibly lethal results.

The battery

Never cause a spark, or allow a naked light, near the vehicle's battery. It will normally be giving off a certain amount of hydrogen gas, which is highly explosive.

Always disconnect the battery earth (ground) terminal before working on the fuel or electrical systems.

If possible, loosen the filler plugs or cover when charging the battery from an external source. Do not charge at an excessive rate or the battery may burst.

Take care when topping up and when carrying the battery. The acid electrolyte, even when diluted, is very corrosive and should not be allowed to contact the eyes or skin.

If you ever need to prepare electrolyte yourself, always add the acid slowly to the water, and never the other way round. Protect against splashes by wearing rubber gloves and goggles.

Mains electricity

When using an electric power tool, inspection light etc which works from the mains, always ensure that the appliance is correctly connected to its plug and that, where necessary, it is properly earthed (grounded). Do not use such appliances in damp conditions and, again, beware of creating a spark or applying excessive heat in the vicinity of fuel or fuel vapour.

Ignition HT voltage

A severe electric shock can result from touching certain parts of the ignition system, such as the HT leads, when the engine is running or being cranked, particularly if components are damp or the insulation is defective. Where an electronic ignition system is fitted, the HT voltage is much higher and could prove fatal.

Routine maintenance

Periodic routine maintenance is a continuous process that begins immediately the machine is used. It must be carried out at specified mileage recordings or on a calendar basis if the machine is not used frequently, whichever is the sooner. Maintenance should always be regarded as an insurance policy, to help keep the machine in the peak of condition and to ensure long, trouble-free service. It has the additional benefit of giving early warning of any faults that may develop and will act as a safety check, to the obvious benefit of both rider and machine alike.

The various maintenance tasks are described under their respective mileage and calander headings. Accompanying diagrams are provided, where necessary. It should be remembered that the interval between the various maintenance tasks serves only as a guide. As the machine gets older or is used under particularly adverse conditions, it is advisable to reduce the intervals between each check.

Some of the tasks are described in detail, where they are not mentioned fully elsewhere in the text. If a specific item is mentioned but not described in detail, it will be covered fully in the appropriate Chapter.

No special tools are required for the normal routine maintenance tasks, the tools found in the average household should suffice.

Pre-ride checks

The following quick checks should be undertaken prior to riding the machine. With a little practice they should become second nature and will only take a few minutes to carry out. Though simple, they will serve to alert the rider of any potentially dangerous or expensive faults.

1. Lift the seat and check the fuel level gauge
2. Check the tyres for obvious signs of damage or low pressure
3. Turn the ignition switch to the 'Test' position and ensure that the oil level lamp comes on
4. Turn the ignition switch to the 'On' position, check that the machine is on its centre stand, then start the engine and allow it to idle
5. Check the operation of the horn, parking lights, head-lamp, indicators and brake light
6. Check that both brakes work and are correctly adjusted
7. Make sure that the oil light is off indicating an adequate supply of oil
8. Check that the throttle operates smoothly and returns to the idle position when released
9. Allow the engine to idle for a few minutes before moving off
10. Check that the mirrors are correctly adjusted and that any luggage is properly secured

If any faults are noted or if further information is required refer to the following pages for detailed Routine Maintenance procedures.

Weekly, or ever 200 miles (300 km)

1 Legal check

Check the operation of the electrical system, ensuring that the lights and horn are working properly and that the lenses are clean. Note that in the UK it is an offence to use a vehicle on which the lights are defective. This applies even when the machine is used during daylight hours. The horn is also a statutory requirement.

Give each tyre a quick visual check for cuts or splits, and check that the depth of tread left is above that required by law.

2 Tyre pressures

Check the tyre pressures. Always check with the tyres cold, using a pressure gauge known to be accurate. It is recommended that a pocket pressure gauge is purchased to offset any fluctuation between garage forecourt instruments. The correct tyre pressures are:-

Front	18 psi (1.25 kg/cm²)
Rear	25 psi (1.75 kg/cm²)

Check tyre pressures using an accurate gauge

3 Control cable lubrication

Apply a few drops of oil to the exposed lengths of inner cable at the tops of the various control cables. This will prevent the cables drying out between the more thorough lubrication given during the six monthly/3000 mile service.

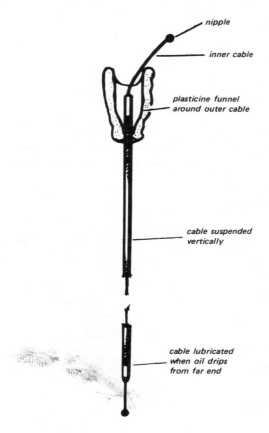

nipple

inner cable

plasticine funnel
around outer cable

cable suspended
vertically

cable lubricated
when oil drips
from far end

Lubricating a control cable

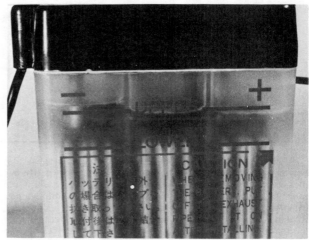

Battery electrolyte level should be kept between lines

Six monthly, or every 3000 miles (5000 km)

Carry out the tasks under the previous headings and complete
the following:

4   Steering and suspension

Check the operation of the front and rear suspension, noting
any stiffness or free play that might have developed. Whilst this
is unlikely, wear will eventually take place and the above
symptoms indicate the need for overhaul. The same is true of
the steering, which should move freely from lock-to-lock. Any
signs of roughness indicates that the bearings are in need of
attention, as does any discernible free play. Reference should
be made to Chapter 4 for further information on the above
items.

5   Checking the battery

Remove the rear carrier and plastic cowl to give access to
the battery. It is housed in a metal tray immediately to the rear
of the seat.

The transparent plastic case of the battery permits the
upper and lower levels of the electrolyte to be observed when
the battery is lifted from its housing below the dual seat.
Maintenance is normally limited to keeping the electrolyte level
between the prescribed upper and lower limits and by making
sure that the vent pipe is not blocked. The lead plates and their
separators can be seen through the transparent case, a further
guide to the general condition of the battery.

Unless acid is spilt, as may occur if the machine falls over,
the electrolyte should always be topped up with distilled water,
to restore the correct level. If acid is spilt on any part of the
machine, it should be neutralised with an alkali such as washing
soda and washed away with plenty of water, otherwise serious
corrosion will occur. Top up with sulphuric acid of the correct
specific gravity (1.260 - 1.280) only when spillage has occured.
Check that the vent pipe is well clear of the frame tubes or any
part of the other cycle parts, for obvious reasons.

1   Sparking plug

Remove the sparking plug, using a proper sparking plug
spanner to avoid any risk of damage to the ceramic insulator.
Examine the colour and condition of the electrodes, comparing
this with the sparking plug condition chart in Chapter 3. This
will give an indication of the general condition of the engine.
Clean the plug electrodes using a wire brush and a small
magneto file or fine emery cloth. If the outer electrode is thin,
or the centre electrode has been eroded excessively, the plug
must be renewed. The gap can be measured with a feeler
gauge, and should be 0.6 to 0.7 mm (0.024 to 0.028 in).

If necessary, adjust the gap by bending the outer electrode.
On no account should any attempt be made to bend the inner
electrode, or damage to the ceramic insulator nose will almost
certainly result. Clean the sparking plug threads and wipe them
with a trace of graphited grease. Refit the plug by hand, then
tighten it carefully with the plug spanner, without over-
tightening.

Sparking plug can be reached after removing side panel

2   Cleaning the air filter

The air filter consists of a moulded plastic casing containing an oil-impregnated foam element. Access to the air filter is gained after the front cowl section immediately below the seat has been removed. This is retained by the two lower side panel screws plus a single control screw. Once the cowl has been removed, pull off the moulded hose which connects the air filter to the carburettor to expose the single screw which secures the air filter cover.

Carefully remove the flat foam element from the casing, taking great care not to tear the foam. The elment can be cleaned by washing it thoroughly in petrol to remove all traces of old oil and accumulated dust. Squeeze out any residual petrol and allow the element to dry before reimpregnating it with clean two-stroke oil. The element should then be wrapped in some clean rag and squeezed to remove any excess oil.

Fit the cleaned and re-oiled element by reversing the dismantling sequence, ensuring that the element fits correctly and that there is no chance of air leakage around it. It should be noted that small two-stroke engines of this type are very sensitive to air filter condition. As the filter becomes choked, the efficiency of the engine will be reduced and fuel consumption will increase. Eventually the engine will begin to run badly, but this will only become evident after the element has become severely choked. It follows that regular cleaning is essential and that the filter condition shoudl be checked whenever poor performance is evident.

3   Check-tighten nuts, bolts and fasteners

Moving in logical sequence around the machine, check to ensure that all nuts, bolts and fasteners are correctly located and secured in position. Retighten any items found to be loose and note their position to ensure they are checked at the next service interval. Ensure all locking devices, such as split-pins, are correctly fitted and in good condition.

This simple check will ensure that the risk of a component becoming detached fom the machine and possibly causing a serious accident to occur is greatly reduced.

4   Carburettor adjustment

Carburettor adjustment should be carried out with the machine on its centre stand and the engine at normal operating temperature. A throttle stop screw and a pilot air screw are provided to allow an even idling speed to be obtained. Start the engine and, using a screwdriver, turn the pilot air screw until the highest possible tick-over speed is obtained. Experimentation should be made by first turning the screw one way and then the other. When the correct position is established, reduce the tick-over speed by turning the throttle stop screw until the engine is running at about 1700 rpm. This is the recommended tick-over speed. The location of both adjustment screws is shown in Chapter 2.

Important note: The automatic transmission system employed on the Passola will engage as the engine speed rises resulting in the rear wheel starting to revolve. Great care must be taken to ensure that there is no risk of the machine running forward. To this end make absolutely certain that the machine is securely positioned on its centre stand and that no tools, rags or other equipment is left near the wheel.

5   Throttle cable adjustment and oil pump synchronization

These two operations must be undertaken jointly because adjustment of either one effects the other. This is because the throttle and oil pump setting are controlled by a single cable from the twistgrip which runs down to a splitter box beneath the floorboard. From here, two cables emerge, one to the carburettor and the other to the oil pump, each having independent adjusters. To maintain the correct oil feed rate for a given engine speed the pump cable must therefore be reset when the throttle cable is adjusted.

The adjustments must be made with the engine at its normal operating temperature. Remove the front cowl beneath the nose of the seat to gain access to the carburettor and oil pump, and remove the plastic cover from the latter. The throttle cable should be adjusted to give 1-2 mm free play before the throttle valve begins to move, and this clearance can be corrected where necessary by means of the adjuster and locknut on the carburettor top.

Once the throttle cable free play has been set it will be necessary to check the pump alignment. Slowly open the thottle twistgrip until all the free play in the throttle cable has been taken up. This is best judged by letting the engine idle and noting the positions at which the engine speed *just* begins to rise. Holding this setting, check that the index mark on the pump pulley is in precise alignment with the projecting pin. If necessary reset the pump cable adjuster to obtain the correct setting. the in-line adjuster is mounted next to the left-hand frame tube, near the air filter assembly.

Remove air cleaner ducting to reveal screw

Lift lid away and remove foam element

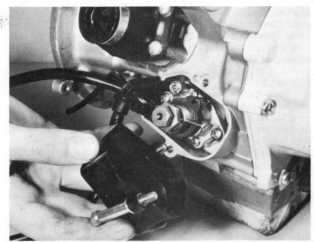

Oil pump location (engine shown removed for clarity)

Oil pump cable has an in-line adjuster (arrowed)

6   Decarbonisation

At the above-mentioned mileage interval it is necessary to remove the cylinder head and the exhaust system so that any accumulated carbon build-up can be removed. It will be necessary to remove the side panels to obtain access to the cylinder head area. Dismantle and remove the exhaust heat shield and the fan cooling ducting around the cylinder.

Note the position of the three pipes which are fitted to the BVS valve on the cylinder head. These should be removed, or alternatively the retainer plate and valve body released from the cylinder head. For further details of the above operations refer to Chapter 1, Section 3 for details of bodywork removal, Section 4 for information on the pipes connected to the BVS valve and Section 7 for details of the cooling ducting arrangement and cylinder head removal. Silencer removal is described in Section 6.

With the cylinder head removed, scrape off all accumulated carbon with a scraper, taking great care not to score the alloy surface below it. It is advantageous to produce as fine a surface finish as possible, and the combustion chamber area may be finished with metal polish if desired. This will leave a surface to which carbon is less likely to cling, and thus the rate of carbon build up will be slowed.

The piston crown should be cleaned in a similar manner, taking great care not to damage it or the cylinder bore. It is a sound precaution to prevent the dislodged carbon from entering the bore by smearing a ring of grease around the edge of the piston before work commences. This will trap the carbon, allowing it to be wiped off with the grease. Again, polishing the piston crown will reduce the subsequent rate of buildup.

When refitting the cylinder head, **always** use a new cylinder head gasket. Fit the head nuts finger tight initially, then tighten them evenly and progressively in a diagonal sequence to prevent warpage. The recommended torque figure is 1.0 kgf m (7.2 lbf ft). Refit the BVS valve or reconnect the pipes, in the latter case making sure that they are fitted to the appropriate stubs. Assemble the fan cowling by reversing the removal order.

The silencer should be renewed and any carbon build-up removal from the exhaust port, exhaust pipe and silencer tailpipe. It should be noted that an obstructed exhaust system will have a marked effect on engine performance.

7   Checking and overhauling the brakes

Remove each wheel in turn and dismantle and clean the brake components. Check the operation of the brake asssembly and apply a trace of grease to the brake cam where it runs in the brake plate. Measure the extent of wear of the linings and renew the shoes as a pair if worn to, or near to, the wear limit. Details will be found in Chapter 5, Sections 3, 4 and 7.

Yearly, or every 6000 miles (10 000 km)

Carry out the service operations listed under the previous headings, then complete the following:

1   Carburettor overhaul

Referring to Chapter 2 for details, remove the carburettor from the machine, then dismantle it for cleaning and inspection. Remove any sediment from the float bowl and clean the jets by blowing them through with compressed air. Check the moving parts for wear or damage and renew these as required. Rebuild the instrument and check the throttle cable, idle speed mixture and oil pump settings as described earlier in Routine Maintenance.

2   Transmission oil change

Obtain a drain tray of about two pints capacity and place it below the drain plug at the rear of the transmission casing. Remove the plug and allow the oil to drain. This operation is greatly facilitated if the engine is warm. Once the old oil has drained completely, clean the plug and sealing washer and renew the latter if necessary. Clean the casing around the drain plug threads, then refit the plug and secure it to a torque setting of 1.5 - 2.0 kgf m (10.9 - 14.5 lbf ft).

Unscrew the filler plug from the upper face of the casing and add 600 cc (21.12 Imp fl oz) of SAE 10W/30 Type SE engine oil. It should be noted that where the transmission casing is dry as the result of overhaul, the oil quantity should be increased to 650 cc (22.88 Imp fl oz). Check the sealing washer on the filler plug and then refit it.

3   Control cable lubrication

The control cable lubrication detail given in the weekly/200 mile service schedule will serve to supplement the full lubrication, which should be carried out as follows.

Disconnect the top of the cable in question, and build up a small funnel of plasticine or similar around the top of the outer cable. Lodge the cable in an upright position, and fill the funnel with light machine oil or engine oil, leave the oil to drain through, preferably overnight.

A quicker and more positive method of lubrication is to use an hydraulic cable oiler which is fairly inexpensive and can be obtained from many motorcycle shops or by mail order from companies advertising in the motorcycle press.

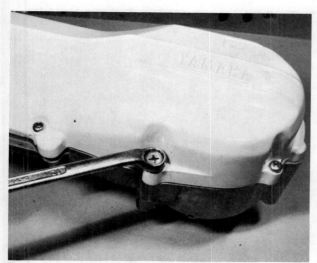

Transmission drain screw is on underside of cover

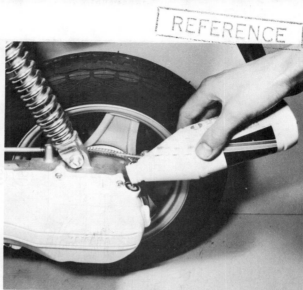

Top up transmission casing with 600 cc of SAE 10W/30

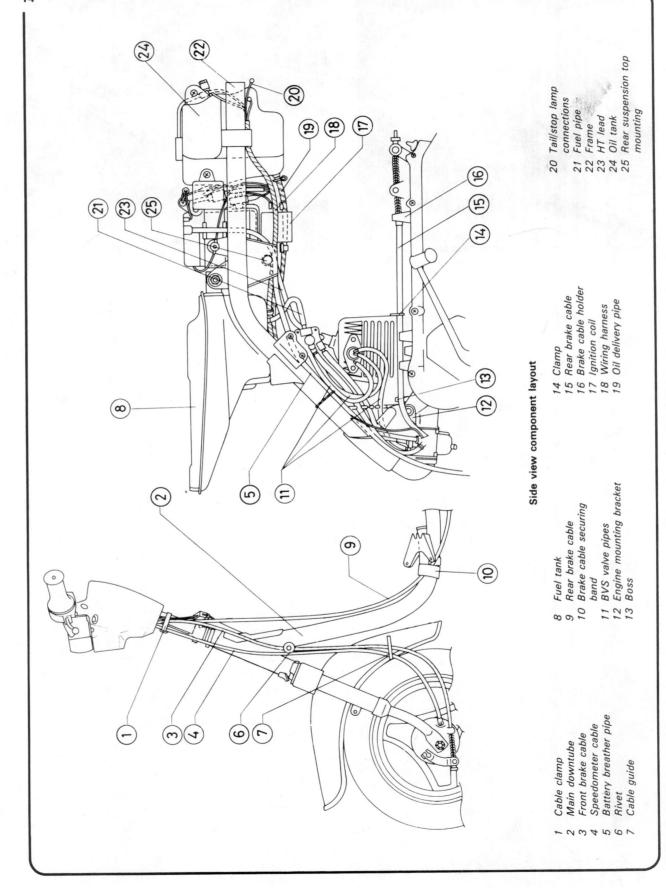

Side view component layout

1 Cable clamp
2 Main downtube
3 Front brake cable
4 Speedometer cable
5 Battery breather pipe
6 Rivet
7 Cable guide

8 Fuel tank
9 Rear brake cable
10 Brake cable securing
   band
11 BVS valve pipes
12 Engine mounting bracket
13 Boss

14 Clamp
15 Rear brake cable
16 Brake cable holder
17 Ignition coil
18 Wiring harness
19 Oil delivery pipe

20 Tail/stop lamp
   connections
21 Fuel pipe
22 Frame
23 HT lead
24 Oil tank
25 Rear suspension top
   mounting

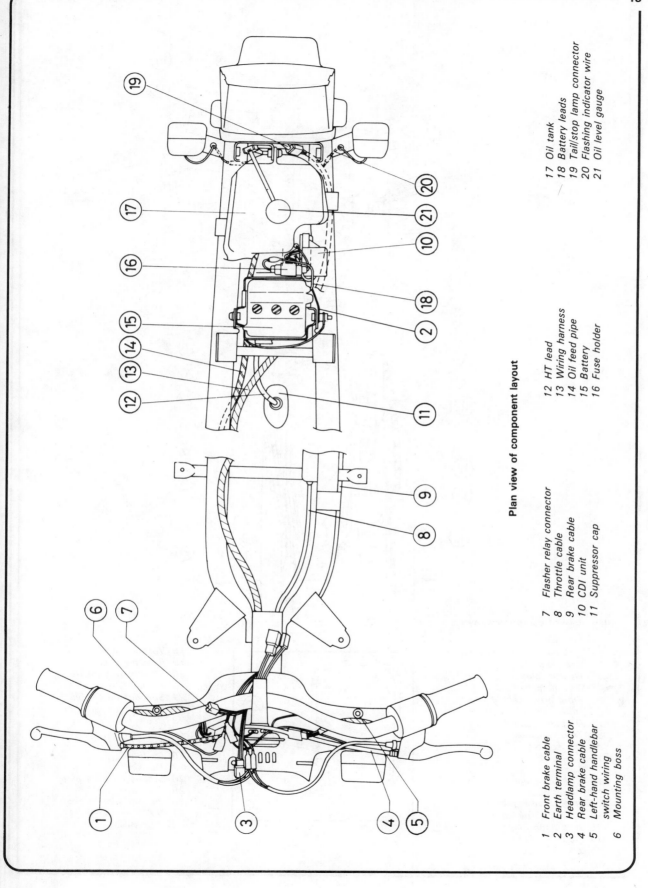

Plan view of component layout

1 Front brake cable
2 Earth terminal
3 Headlamp connector
4 Rear brake cable
5 Left-hand handlebar
   switch wiring
6 Mounting boss

7 Flasher relay connector
8 Throttle cable
9 Rear brake cable
10 CDI unit
11 Suppressor cap

12 HT lead
13 Wiring harness
14 Oil feed pipe
15 Battery
16 Fuse holder

17 Oil tank
18 Battery leads
19 Tail/stop lamp connector
20 Flashing indicator wire
21 Oil level gauge

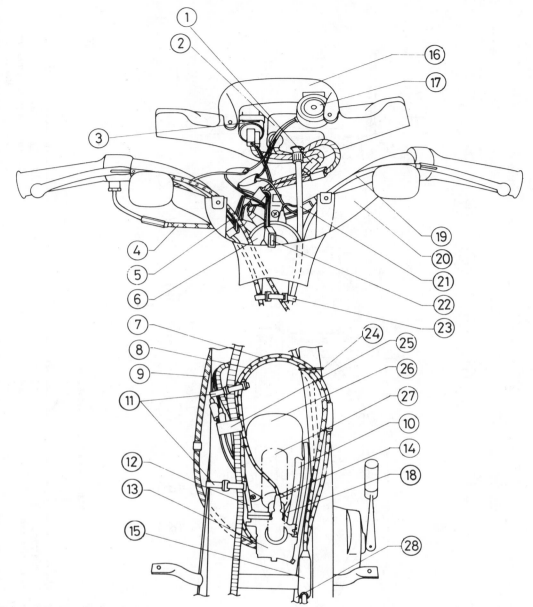

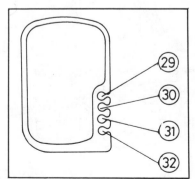

Plan view of component layout

1 Ignition switch connector
2 Speedometer
3 Flasher relay
4 Throttle cable
5 Front brake cable
6 Horn
7 Oil pump cable
8 Throttle cable
9 Oil feed pipe
10 Fuel pipe
11 Cable tie
12 CDI and magneto wires
13 Carburettor
14 BVS valve pipe
15 Cable splitter box
16 Instrument panel
17 Audio – pilot (not UK models)

18 Vacuum pipe
19 Rear brake cable
20 Instrument panel lower section
21 Speedometer cable
22 Headlamp connector
23 Cable tie
24 Guide
25 Tape
26 Air filter
27 Trunking
28 Battery breather pipe
29 Fuel pipe
30 Vacuum pipe
31 N/A
32 BVS valve

YAMAHA PASSOLA

Check list

Pre-ride checks

1   Lift the seat and check the fuel level gauge
2   Check the tyres for damage and low tyre pressure
3   Turn the ignition switch to the 'Test' position and check that the oil level lamp comes on
4   Turn the ignition switch to the 'On' position, with the machine on its centre stand and start the engine, allowing it to idle
5   Check the horn, parking lights, headlamps, indicators and brake light for correct operation
6   Check the operation of the brakes and that they are correctly adjusted
7   Make sure that the oil light is off indicating an adequate supply of oil
8   Check that the throttle operates smoothly and returns to the idle position when released
9   Allow the engine to idle for a few minutes before moving off
10 Check that the mirrors are correctly adjusted and that any luggage is properly secured

Weekly or every 200 miles (300 km)

1   Check the operation of the electrical system
2   Check the tyre pressures
3   Lubricate the exposed parts of control cables
4   Check for stiffness or play in the steering and suspension
5   Check the battery electrolyte level

Six monthly or every 3000 miles (5000 km)

1   Clean and adjust the sparking plug
2   Clean the air filter element
3   Check and if necessary tighten any loose bolts, nuts and fasteners
4   Adjust the carburettor
5   Adjust the throttle cable and synchronise the oil pump
6   Decarbonise the cylinder head and piston crown
7   Overhaul the brakes

Yearly or every 6000 miles (10 000 km)

1   Dismantle and clean the carburettor
2   Change the transmission oil
3   Lubricate the control cables

Adjustment data

Tyre pressures
Front   18 psi (1.25 kg/cm^2)
Rear   25 psi (1.75 kg/cm^2)

Sparking plug type
NGK   BP 4HS
Champion   L86C
Nippondenso   W14FP-UL
Sparking plug gap   0.6 – 0.7 mm (0.024 – 0.028 in)

Ignition timing   21° BTDC à 5000 rpm (non-adjustable)

Engine idle speed   1700 rpm

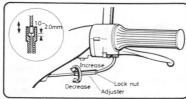

Increase
Decrease
Lock nut
Adjuster

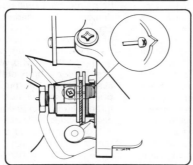

Recommended lubricants

Component	Quantity	Type/viscosity
① Engine	As required	Yamaha Autolube or equivalent two-stroke oil
② Transmission	600 cc (21.12 Imp fl oz)	SAE 10W/30 SE motor oil
③ Steering head bearings	As required	Medium weight general purpose grease
④ Wheel bearings	As required	High melting point grease
⑤ Throttle twist grip	As required	Lithium-based grease
⑥ Controls and pivots	As required	Medium weight general purpose grease
⑦ General lubrication	As required	SAE 10W/30 SE motor oil

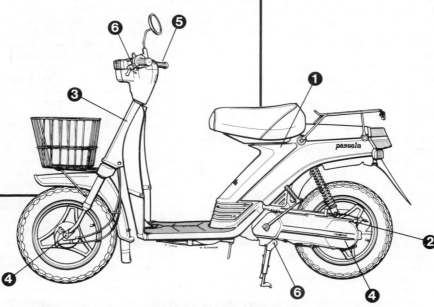

ROUTINE MAINTENANCE GUIDE

Tools and working facilities

The first priority when undertaking maintenance or repair work of any sort on a motorcycle is to have a clean, dry, well-lit working area. Work carried out in peace and quiet in the well-ordered atmosphere of a good workshop will give more satisfaction and much better results than can usually be achieved in poor working conditions. A good workshop must have a clean flat workbench or a solidly constructed table of convenient working height. The workbench or table should be equipped with a vice which has a jaw opening of at least 4 in (100 mm). A set of jaw covers should be made from soft metal such as aluminium alloy or copper, or from wood. These covers will minimise the marking or damaging of soft or delicate components which may be clamped in the vice. Some clean, dry, storage space will be required for tools, lubricants and dismantled components. It will be necessary during a major overhaul to lay out engine/gearbox components for examination and to keep them where they will remain undisturbed for as long as is necessary. To this end it is recommended that a supply of metal or plastic containers of suitable size is collected. A supply of clean, lint-free, rags for cleaning purposes and some newspapers, other rags, or paper towels for mopping up spillages should also be kept. If working on a hard concrete floor note that both the floor and one's knees can be protected from oil spillages and wear by cutting open a large cardboard box and spreading it flat on the floor under the machine or workbench. This also helps to provide some warmth in winter and to prevent the loss of nuts, washers, and other tiny components which have a tendency to disappear when dropped on anything other than a perfectly clean, flat, surface.

Unfortunately, such working conditions are not always available to the home mechanic. When working in poor conditions it is essential to take extra time and care to ensure that the components being worked on are kept scrupulously clean and to ensure that no components or tools are lost or damaged.

A selection of good tools is a fundamental requirement for anyone contemplating the maintenance and repair of a motor vehicle. For the owner who does not possess any, their purchase will prove a considerable expense, offsetting some of the savings made by doing-it-yourself. However, provided that the tools purchased are of good quality, they will last for many years and prove an extremely worthwhile investment.

To help the average owner to decide which tools are needed to carry out the various tasks detailed in this manual, we have compiled three lists of tools under the following headings: *Maintenance and minor repair, Repair and overhaul,* and *Specialized.* The newcomer to practical mechanics should start off with the simpler jobs around the vehicle. Then, as his confidence and experience grow, he can undertake more difficult tasks, buying extra tools as and when they are needed.

In this way, a *Maintenance and minor repair* tool kit can be built-up into a *Repair and overhaul* tool kit over a considerable period of time without any major cash outlays. The experienced home mechanic will have a tool kit good enough for most repair and overhaul procedures and will add tools from the specialized category when he feels the expense is justified by the amount of use these tools will be put to.

It is obviously not possible to cover the subject of tools fully here. For those who wish to learn more about tools and their use there is a book entitled *How to Choose and Use Car Tools* available from the publishers of this manual. Although, as its title implies, this publication is directed at car owners, the information given is equally applicable to motorcycle owners. It also provides an introduction to basic workshop practice which will be of interest to a home mechanic working on any type of motor vehicle.

As a general rule, it is better to buy the more expensive, good quality tools. Given reasonable use, such tools will last for a very long time, whereas the cheaper, poor quality, item will wear out faster and need to be renewed more often, thus nullifying the original saving. There is also the risk of a poor quality tool breaking while in use, causing personal injury or expensive damage to the component being worked on. It should be noted, however, that many car accessory shops and the large department stores sell tools of reasonable quality at competitive prices. The best example of this is found with socket sets, where a medium-priced socket set will be quite adequate for the home owner and yet prove less expensive than a selection of individual sockets and accessories. This is because individual pieces are usually only available from expensive, top quality, ranges and whilst they are undeniably good, it should be remembered that they are intended for professional use.

The basis of any toolkit is a set of spanners. While open-ended spanners with their slim jaws, are useful for working on awkwardly-positioned nuts, ring spanners have advantages in that they grip the nut far more positively. There is less risk of the spanner slipping off the nut and damaging it, for this reason alone ring spanners are to be preferred. Ideally, the home mechanic should acquire a set of each, but if expense rules this out a set of combination spanners (open-ended at one end and with a ring of the same size at the other) will provide a good compromise. Another item which is so useful it should be considered an essential requirement for any home mechanic is a set of socket spanners. These are available in a variety of drive sizes. It is recommended that the $\frac{1}{2}$-inch drive type is purchased to begin with as although bulkier and more expensive than the $\frac{3}{8}$-inch type, the larger size is far more common and will accept a greater variety of torque wrenches, extension pieces and socket sizes. The socket set should comprise sockets of sizes between 8 and 24 mm, a reversible ratchet drive, an extension bar of about 10 inches in length, a spark plug socket with a rubber insert, and a universal joint. Other attachments can be added to the set at a later date.

Maintenance and minor repair tool kit

Set of spanners 8 – 24 mm
Set of sockets and attachments
Spark plug spanner with rubber insert – 10, 12, or 14 mm as appropriate
Adjustable spanner
C-spanner/pin spanner
Torque wrench (same size drive as sockets)
Set of screwdrivers (flat blade)
Set of screwdrivers (cross-head)
Set of Allen keys 4 – 10 mm
Impact screwdriver and bits
Ball pein hammer – 2 lb
Hacksaw (junior)
Self-locking pliers – Mole grips or vice grips
Pliers – combination
Pliers – needle nose
Wire brush (small)
Soft-bristled brush
Tyre pump
Tyre pressure gauge
Tyre tread depth gauge
Oil can
Fine emery cloth
Funnel (medium size)
Drip tray
Grease gun
Set of feeler gauges
Strobe timing light
Continuity tester (dry battery and bulb)
Soldering iron and solder
Wire stripper or craft knife
PVC insulating tape
Assortment of split pins, nuts, bolts, and washers

Repair and overhaul toolkit

The tools in this list are virtually essential for anyone undertaking major repairs to a motorcycle and are additional to the tools listed above. Concerning Torx driver bits, Torx screws are encountered on some of the more modern machines where their use is restricted to fastening certain components inside the engine/gearbox unit. It is therefore recommended that if Torx bits cannot be borrowed from a local dealer, they are purchased individually as the need arises. They are not in regular use in the motor trade and will therefore only be available in specialist tool shops.

Plastic or rubber soft-faced mallet
Torx driver bits
Pliers – electrician's side cutters
Circlip pliers – internal (straight or right-angled tips are available)
Circlip pliers – external
Cold chisel
Centre punch
Pin punch
Scriber
Scraper (made from soft metal such as aluminium or copper)
Soft metal drift
Steel rule/straight edge
Assortment of files
Electric drill and bits
Wire brush (large)
Soft wire brush (similar to those used for cleaning suede shoes)
Sheet of plate glass
Hacksaw (large)
Stud extractor set (E-Z out)

Specialized tools

This is not a list of the tools made by the machine's manufacturer to carry out a specific task on a limited range of models. Occasional references are made to such tools in the text of this manual and, in general, an alternative method of carrying out the task without the manufacturer's tool is given where possible. The tools mentioned in this list are those which are not used regularly and are expensive to buy in view of their infrequent use. Where this is the case it may be possible to hire or borrow the tools against a deposit from a local dealer or tool hire shop. An alternative is for a group of friends or a motorcycle club to join in the purchase.

Piston ring compressor
Universal bearing puller
Cylinder bore honing attachment (for electric drill)
Micrometer set
Vernier calipers
Dial gauge set
Cylinder compression gauge
Multimeter
Dwell meter/tachometer

Care and maintenance of tools

Whatever the quality of the tools purchased, they will last much longer if cared for. This means in practice ensuring that a tool is used for its intended purpose; for example screwdrivers should not be used as a substitute for a centre punch, or as chisels. Always remove dirt or grease and any metal particles but remember that a light film of oil will prevent rusting if the tools are infrequently used. The common tools can be kept together in a large box or tray but the more delicate, and more expensive, items should be stored separately where they cannot be damaged. When a tool is damaged or worn out, be sure to renew it immediately. It is false economy to continue to use a worn spanner or screwdriver which may slip and cause expensive damage to the component being worked on.

Fastening systems

Fasteners, basically, are nuts, bolts and screws used to hold two or more parts together. There are a few things to keep in mind when working with fasteners. Almost all of them use a locking device of some type; either a lock washer, lock nut, locking tab or thread adhesive. All threaded fasteners should be clean, straight, have undamaged threads and undamaged corners on the hexagon head where the spanner fits. Develop the habit of replacing all damaged nuts and bolts with new ones.

Rusted nuts and bolts should be treated with a rust penetrating fluid to ease removal and prevent breakage. After applying the rust penetrant, let it 'work' for a few minutes before trying to loosen the nut or bolt. Badly rusted fasteners may have to be chiseled off or removed with a special nut breaker, available at tool shops.

Flat washers and lock washers, when removed from an assembly should always be replaced exactly as removed. Replace any damaged washers with new ones. Always use a flat washer between a lock washer and any soft metal surface (such as aluminium), thin sheet metal or plastic. Special lock nuts can only be used once or twice before they lose their locking ability and must be renewed.

If a bolt or stud breaks off in an assembly, it can be drilled out and removed with a special tool called an E-Z out. Most dealer service departments and motorcycle repair shops can perform this task, as well as others (such as the repair of threaded holes that have been stripped out).

Chapter 1 Engine and transmission

For information and revisions to later models, see Chapter 7

Contents

Specifications

Engine

Type	Air cooled two-stroke, single cylinder
Porting	Piston and reed valve
Capacity	49 cc (3.0 cu in)
Bore	40 mm (1.575 in)
Stroke	39.2 mm (1.543 in)
Compression ratio	6.4 : 1
Lubrication	Metered pump system (Yamaha Autolube)

Piston

Type	Aluminium alloy
Piston to bore clearance	0.024 – 0.035 mm (0.0009 – 0.0012 in)
Piston oversizes	+0.25, +0.50 mm (+0.0098, +0.0197 in)

Piston rings

Type	Keystone
End gap (installed)	0.15 – 0.35 mm (0.0059 – 0.0138 in)

Cylinder barrel

Type	Cast iron
Standard bore size	40 mm (1.575 in)
Taper limit	0.05 mm (0.002 in)
Ovality limit	0.01 mm (0.0004 in)

Crankshaft assembly

Runout (maximum)	0.03 mm (0.0012 in)
Big-end side clearance	0.3 – 0.6 mm (0.0118 – 0.0236 in)
Service limit	1.0 mm (0.0394 in)
Deflection at small-end	0.8 – 1.0 mm (0.0315 – 0.0394 in)
Service limit	2.0 mm (0.0787 in)
Main bearing type	6203 (2 off)
Small-end bearing	Caged needle roller
Big-end bearing	Needle roller
LH crankshaft oil seal	SD-23-35-7
RH crankshaft oil seal	SD-17-35-7

Clutch

Type	Automatic, centrifugal
Lining thickness	2.3 – 2.4 mm (0.0906 – 0.0945 in)
Clutch spring free length	29.6 mm (1.1654 in)
Service limit	30.0 mm (1.1811 mm)
Clutch operation starts @	2700 rpm
Clutch fully engaged @	3600 rpm
Gear changes @	4900 rpm

Transmission

Type	Automatic two-speed incorporating chain drive to rear stub axle. Engine transmission and final drive built in unit
Primary reduction ratio	2.357 : 1 (33/14)
Secondary reduction type	Gear, 2-speed
Gear selection	Automatic
Gear ratios:	
1st	6.454 : 1 (71/11)
2nd	4.400 : 1 (66/15)

Note: Non UK models are equipped with single speed transmission having a ratio of 5.583 : 1 (67/12)

Torque wrench settings

	kgf m	lbf ft
Cylinder head nuts	1.0	7.2
Flywheel rotor	4.3	31.1
Reed valve	1.0	7.2
Air filter	1.0	7.2
Exhaust pipe	1.0	7.2
Silencer mounting	1.8	13.0
Crankcase and cover	1.0	7.2
Drain bolt	1.8	13.0
Clutch	3.0	21.7
Chain tensioner	1.0	7.2
Swinging arm pivot	4.5	32.5
Suspension unit bolt:		
Lower	1.8	13.0
Upper	2.3	16.6
Rear wheel nut	6.0	43.4

1 General description

The engine/transmission unit of the Passola has been designed to be unobtrusive, and is well hidden in normal use. In this respect it is quite unlike conventional motorcycles or mopeds derived from motorcycles, and it resembles more closely the current Italian scooter and moped designs. The engine unit itself is a vertical single-cylinder two-stroke with reed valve induction and pump-fed lubrication. It is built in unit with the primary drive casing and transmission assembly, forming a horizontal structural unit which is pivoted at the front to act as a swinging arm.

The crankcase is formed by two aluminium alloy castings, the left-hand half being extended to act as the transmission casing and house the transmission clutches and primary chain.

The crankshaft is supported by two journal ball main bearings. The outer face of the right-hand crankcase half houses the flywheel generator and electronic ignition components, the flywheel rotor being keyed to the tapered crankshaft end. Lugs at the front of the crankcase halves house the bearings upon which the unit is suspended in the frame.

On the left-hand end of the crankshaft a centrifugal automatic clutch transmits drive to the primary chain to a driven sprocket. At low speeds drive is transmitted through a ratchet to the rear wheel, whilst at higher speeds a second centrifugal clutch transmits drive through the 2nd gear pinions, the ratchet disconnecting the low ratio drive. In the case of single speed models supplied to most European countries a single speed arrangement is employed, and the second clutch and 2nd gear pinions are omitted. Starting on all models is by a ratchet and segment kick start system.

2   Operations with the engine/transmission unit in the frame

As mentioned earlier, the engine/transmission unit is well hidden when installed in the frame and this can make the removal of many of the ancillary parts rather difficult, though not impossible. The items listed below can be removed or worked on without having to resort to the removal of the entire unit, although it may prove easier to do so. Whichever approach is adopted it will be necessary to remove some or all of the surrounding bodywork.

1   Fan cowlings
2   Cylinder head
3   Cylinder barrel and piston
4   Flywheel rotor and stator
5   Air cleaner
6   Carburettor
7   Kickstart mechanism
8   Transmission components
9   Oil pump

If attention to the crankshaft assembly, big-end or main bearings or the crankcases is necessary, it will be necessary to remove the entire unit before separation is possible. If a number of the operations listed above are to be carried out it may prove advantageous to remove the unit to gain better access.

3   Bodywork: removal and refitting

1   It will be necessary to remove some or all of the body panels to gain access to the engine/transmission suspension and electrical components. It was found in practice that it is advisable to remove most of the panels to gain better working clearance and to obviate the risk of damage to the paintwork. The various panels and the items that they conceal are listed below.

Rear cowl and luggage rack
2   The cowl is fitted to the rear of the seat and below the luggage rack, both of which should be removed to gain unrestricted access to the oil tank, battery, fuses and many of the electrical connectors. To remove it, lift the seat and unscrew the two wing bolts at the front. The cowl can now be lifted and pulled forward and clear of the luggage rack. The rack is secured by two domed nuts at the front and by two bolts at the rear. The right-hand front stay has a slotted end to facilitate removal and a plain washer is fitted beneath its nut. A 12 mm spanner will release the nuts and the bolts.

Side panels
3   The side panels run from the front cowl and floorboards to the rear lamp unit, and conceal most of the engine/transmission assembly, the rectifier and ignition coil and the vacuum-operated fuel tap. Each panel is secured by the rack mounting bolt and nut and by a screw which passes into the front edge via a hole in the front cowl.

Front cowl
4   This is a two-piece component covering the area below the seat nose and containing the air filter assembly and the carburettor. The two parts of the cowl are riveted together and thus are removed as one. The panel is retained by the two front side panel screws plus a single central screw near the top.

Footboard
5   The pressed steel footboard is secured by four bolts passing into captive nuts on the support arms and by three screws to the lower edge of the legshield. Its removal allows better access to the front of the engine unit and uncovers the throttle/oil pump cable junction box. To reach the mounting bolts the floormat should be pulled away from its location holes.

Legshield
6   The legshield does not affect work on the engine, but can be removed to give better access after the floorboard/legshield screws have been released. It is retained by a single central screw to the steering column. The small steering column cover is a push fit on its three mounting lugs, but need not be disturbed.
7   The various body panels can be fitted in the reverse order of dismantling, starting with the legshield and working back. When fitting screws which thread directly into plastic take care to avoid overtightening and ensure that any headed spacers are fitted correctly. The footboard bolts are prone to corrosion and should be greased before installation, preferably with a copper-based grease designed to ease subsequent removal.

3.2a A: Rear cowl wingbolt B: Rack and side panel bolt

3.2b The rear cowl section can be removed with rack in place

3.3 Side panel is retained at three points (arrowed)

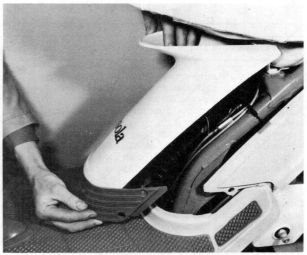

3.4 Front cowl section is secured by three screws

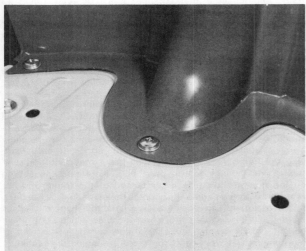

3.5a Remove rubber mat and release legshield screws ...

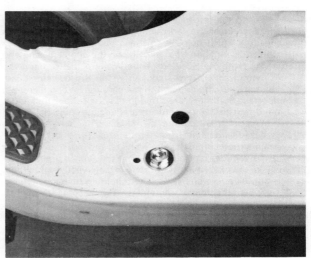

3.5b ... then unscrew the four footboard bolts

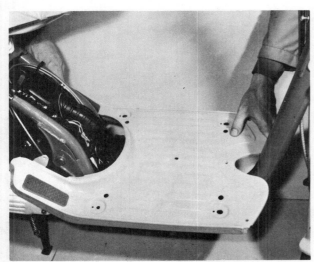

3.5c Footboard can now be lifted away from frame

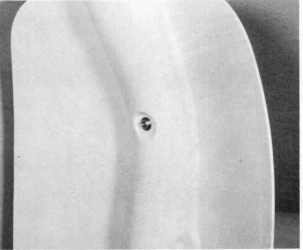

3.6 Legshield is now secured by a single screw

4   Removing the engine/transmission unit from the frame

1   Place the machine on its centre stand, allowing plenty of working space on each side and to the front. Where possible, it is helpful to place the machine on a stout raised platform so that it is about two feet above floor level. This is not essential but will reduce the amount of stooping that will otherwise be required. Most of the dismantling work can be carried out unaided, but an assistant should be available during the latter stages when it will be necessary to lift the frame assembly clear of the engine unit. The various body panels should be removed as described in Section 3 of this Chapter.

2   Trace the flywheel generator leads backs to the four pin connector on the right-hand side of the air cleaner casing, releasing the cable clips which hold the wiring to the frame. Release the connector and separate the single black/red lead which lies next to it. Pull off the high tension (HT) lead at the sparking plug and lodge the plug cap clear of the engine.

3   Remove the rear mudguard by pushing it forward until the mounting lugs clear the frame. Once it has been unclipped the mudguard can be manoeuvred clear of the rear wheel and removed.

4   Moving to the left-hand side of the machine, remove the left-hand section of the fan ducting by unscrewing the single retaining bolt which holds it to the cylinder head. The lower edge can be disengaged from the lugs on the engine casing and lifted away. Note the position of the vacuum fuel tap and the BVS (Bimetal vacuum switching) valve on the cylinder head. Pipes run between the two and to the carburettor and oil pump. It is important that these are fitted in the correct position and it was found that to avoid confusion the vacuum fuel tap should be removed from the frame by releasing its two mounting screws, but left attached to the carburettor.

5   Obtain a metal drain can, then pull off the fuel pipe from the tank to the vacuum fuel tap and allow the fuel to drain. While the fuel is draining make a sketch of the vacuum fuel tap, carburettor, oil pump and BVS valve, showing the pipe connections between the four components. The accompanying line drawing illustrates the position of each hose on the machine used in the workshop project, but there may be some variation on earlier or subsequent versions. It will be noted that the three hoses to the BVS valve are printed along their length with the letters A, B or C to denote their purpose. This makes reassembly

rather more straightforward than might otherwise be the case.

6   It will be found that some of the hoses are routed above the front engine mounting and some below it, which means that it will be necessary to remove some of them prior to engine removal. Though not essential, it was decided to remove the carburettor and vacuum fuel tap as an assembly, leaving the BVS valve and the oil pump in position. Start by pulling off the air cleaner hose from the casing and at the carburettor intake. Release the air cleaner mounting screws and lift the plastic casing away. Release the single screw which secures the carburettor top and withdraw the throttle valve assembly. This can be left attached to the cable and lodged clear of the engine.

7   Remove the plastic oil pump cover by releasing its plain and extended mounting bolts. Lift the cover away, then free the cable by disengaging it from the pump pulley and anchor point. Trace the small oil delivery pipe up fom the pump and pull it off at the carburettor stub, taking care not to lose the small cylindrical spring clip from its end. Release the carburettor mounting clamp and free the instrument from its rubber mounting adaptor. As it is lifted away, disconnect the hoses to the vacuum fuel tap where they would otherwise impede removal, refitting them as soon as the assembly is clear of the frame. The marked (A,B and C) pipes should be freed at the BVS valve on the cylinder head, having noted the correct position of each.

8   Slacken and remove the rear brake adjuster nut, then displace the cable from its trunnion and from the stop on the casing. Remove the trunnion from the brake arm and refit it on the threaded cable end with the spring, retaining both with the adjuster nut for safe keeping. Free the cable from its guides along the chain case.

9   The engine can now be removed, or more accurately, the chassis can be lifted clear of the power unit. The latter will remain standing on the wheel and centre stand, but an assistant should be on hand to help manoeuvre the light but unweildly frame assembly clear. With one person supporting and steadying the frame, free the suspension lower mounting bolt, and the engine (swinging arm) pivot bolt. Note that the sprung engine mount should be left attached to the frame and not removed with the engine. As soon as the pivot shaft is freed the frame assembly can be lifted away. As this happens, check carefully for any electrical or control cables which might have caught on the engine unit. The frame can be placed out of harm's way and work can commence on engine dismantling.

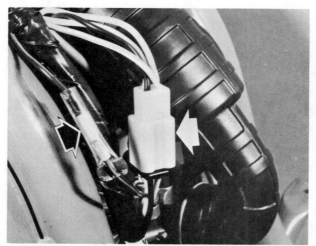

4.2 Disconnect single bullet connector and multiway connector

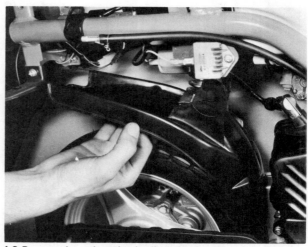

4.3 Rear mudguard section is clipped to frame

4.4a Note BVS hose connections before removal of fuel tap

4.4b Vacuum tap is suitably inscribed with hose letters

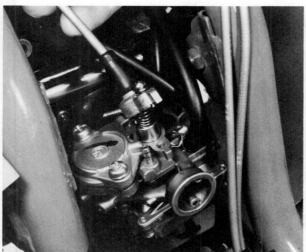

4.6 Release carburettor top and throttle valve assembly

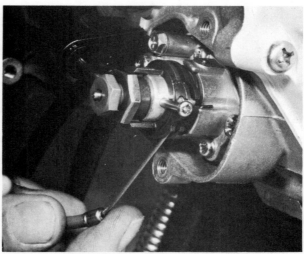

4.7 Oil pump cable should be disconnected from pulley

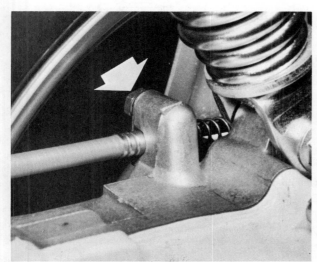

4.8 Single bolt clamps rear brake outer cable

4.9 Frame assembly can be lifted clear of engine unit

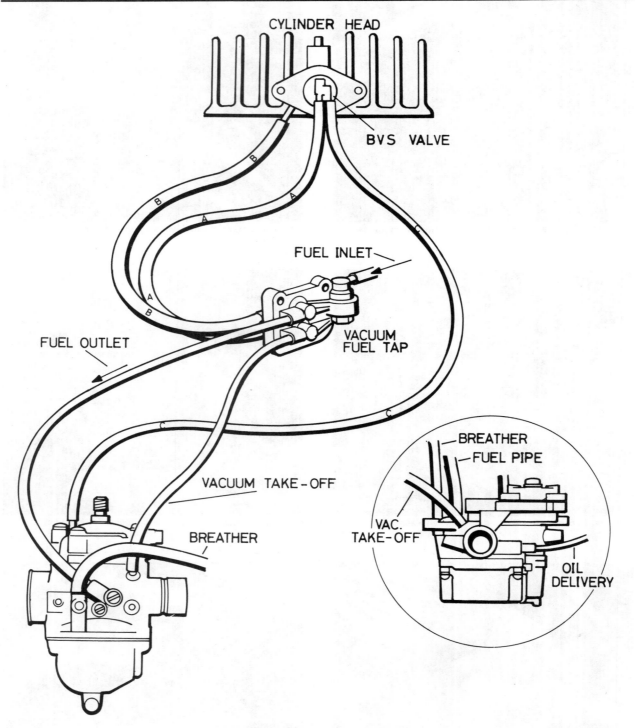

Fig. 1.1 BVS valve pipe connections

5   Dismantling the engine/transmission unit: general

1   Having removed the engine/transmission unit as an assembly as described in Section 4 of this Chapter it can be placed on the workbench in readiness for further dismantling. The centre stand and rear wheel can be left in position at this stage and will provide a convenient and stable support for the unit. It is, however, important that cleaning solvents are kept away from the rear tyre which would otherwise be damaged by them.

2   Before commencing work on the engine unit, the external surfaces should be cleaned thoroughly. A motorcycle engine has very little protection from road grit and other foreign matter, which will finds its way into the dismantled engine if this simple

precaution is not taken. One of the proprietary cleaning compounds, such as 'Gunk' or 'Jizer' can be used to good effect, particularly if the compound is worked into the film of oil and grease before it is washed away. Special care is necessary, when washing down to prevent water from entering any exposed parts of the engine unit.

3   Never use undue force to remove any stubborn part unless specific mention is made of this requirement. There is invariably good reason why a part is difficult to remove, often because the dismantling operation has been tackled in the wrong sequence.

4   It should be noted at this juncture that a service tool will be required to remove the flywheel rotor from the crankshaft taper. The part number of this tool is 90890-01189. This tool may be purchased through an authorised Yamaha Service Agent but in view of the infrequency of its use it is unlikely that it will be worthwhile buying it. If the owner is on good terms with his local Yamaha agent, then the agent may be persuaded to lend or hire the tool over the weekend when he is unlikely to need it himself. Alternatively, the engine may be taken to the Service Agent and he can then remove the flywheel rotor. Prior arrangement should be made for this to be done. It is our experience that the service tool is absolutely essential. There is no safe alternative method of removing the rotor.

5   No further service tools will be necessary, but an impact driver should be considered essential for removing the numerous cross-headed screws. Many of these will be sufficiently tight to resist any other method of removal.

6   Dismantling the engine/transmission unit: removing the silencer

1   Remove the three screws which retain the exhaust heat shield to the silencer body, noting the heat resistant fibre washers and the tubular spacer on the front screw. Lift the heat shield away, then remove the two silencer mounting bolts at the front edge of the unit. The silencer is now retained by two bolts at the exhaust port flange.

2   If the unit is on the workbench it should be tipped on its side to give better access to the recessed bolts. A similar procedure will be necessary if the operation is being undertaken with the engine installed. Using a 10 mm socket on a long extension slacken the two flange bolts by about 3 or 4 turns. Note that the flange is slotted, and it is therefore unnecessary to remove the bolts completely. Once slack, the silencer should be rocked to break the exhaust port seal. The silencer can now be pulled rearwards to clear the flange bolts and lifted away.

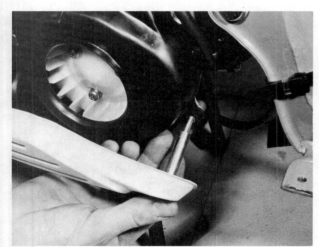

6.1 Note tubular spacer on front heat shield screw

7   Dismantling the engine/transmission unit: removing the cylinder head, barrel and piston

1   Before the above components can be removed it will be necessary to dismantle the component parts of the fan cooling ducting which surrounds them. This can be accomplished with the engine in or out of the frame, noting that in the former case it will be necessary to remove the front cowl and side panels as described in Section 3, followed by the air cleaner assembly as described in paragraph 6 of Section 4. It is possible to dismantle the cylinder head, barrel and piston with the air cleaner in position, but access is rather restricted.

2   The large plastic cowl on the right-hand (fan) side of the unit is retained by a total of three screws, two of which also secure the exhaust heat shield. If the latter is still in position it should be removed (see Section 6) and the remaining cowl screw released. The cowl can now be lifted away. The smaller plastic cowl on the left-hand (drive) side will probably have been removed at this stage, but if not can be lifted away after the single retaining screw has been removed.

3   If it is still in position, remove the rubber flap from the front edge of the metal centre section of the ducting. The ducting can be removed after its two mounting bolts have been released from the rear edge of the crankcase. Lift the metal section away to expose the cylinder head and barrel.

4   Slacken the four cylinder head nuts evenly and in a diagonal sequence, turning each one by about $\frac{1}{4}$ turn at a time to prevent warpage of the light alloy cylinder head casting. Once pressure has been released, the nuts can be run off the holding studs and the head lifted away. It is unlikely that there will be any tendency for the cylinder head to remain stuck to the barrel face, but should this problem arise a few judicious taps around the edge using a soft-faced mallet should succeed in breaking the joint. Note that the washers beneath the cylinder head nuts will drop free and should be retained whilst the cylinder head gasket should be removed and discarded.

5   The cylinder barrel is removed by sliding it off the holding studs. It may prove necessary to break the seal between the cylinder base and crankcase by rocking the cylinder barrel. Once free, lift the barrel by about 1 inch (25 mm) and push some clean rag into the crankcase mouth to prevent the ingress of any debris that might be released when the piston emerges from its bore. The barrel can now be lifted clear and placed to one side.

6   Leave the rag packing in the crankcase mouth until the piston has been removed. The piston is supported on a gudgeon pin which is held in place by a wire circlip at each end of the piston bore. The circlips can be removed by grasping the projecting tang with the pointed-nose pliers and pulling the clip from its groove. This will strain the clips and for this reason they should be renewed as a precaution against their subsequent failure. Once the clips have been removed the piston can be freed by pushing the gudgeon pin from its bore. The pin is usually a light sliding fit and easily removed, but if it appears stuck it can be released as follows.

7   Obtain a container of boiling water in which some rag has been placed. Taking care to avoid scalding, wrap the rag around the piston and leave it for about a minute. The alloy piston will expand much faster than the steel gudgeon pin, which will now push out quite easily.

8   Should it ever prove necessary, a drawbolt extractor can be used to remove the gudgeon pin. See the accompanying figure. Never attempt to drift the pin out because there is a real risk of danger to the connecting rod or bearings. As the piston is removed retrieve the caged needle small-end bearing. Note the arrow mark on the piston crown – this must face the exhaust port when the piston is refitted.

8   Dismantling the engine/transmission unit: removing the flywheel generator

1   Access to the flywheel generator is gained after removing the right-hand fan cowling. It should be noted before any attempt is made to remove the rotor that a threaded extractor, Yamaha part number 90890-01189, should be considered essential. Alternative methods were tried on the machine featured in this manual, but in every case there was a likelihood of damage resulting from the use of improvised tools, so the attempt was abandoned. The tool can be ordered from a Yamaha Service Agent or alternatively the partly dismantled unit can be taken in for rotor removal.

2   Remove the three screws which retain the fan to the rotor and lift it away. When slackening the rotor securing nut and when using the extractor, it will be necessary to contrive a method of preventing the crankshaft from turning. If the cylinder head, barrel and piston have been removed it is permissible to pass a smooth round bar through the connecting rod small-end eye, supporting its ends on small wooden blocks to avoid damaging the crankcase.

3   If the rotor is to be removed with the rest of the unit assembled, a holding tool must be borrowed or made up. Note that the automatic clutches preclude any other method of locking the crankshaft. The Yamaha magneto holding tool, part

number 90890-01235 is ideal for the purpose but is not really worth buying for home use. If it cannot be borrowed a simple but effective alternative can be made up using a length of steel strip with a hole drilled at one end and a second hole about $3\frac{1}{2}$ inches from it. Suitable bolts and nuts can be fixed in the holes, and the protruding ends engaged in the slots in the rotor face to hold it in position.

4   With the rotor immobilised in this fashion the central retaining nut can be removed, as can the plain washer which fits below it. The rotor extractor is screwed into the large internal thread in the rotor boss. Once in position, tighten the extractor bolt to draw the rotor off the crankshaft taper. It is likely that the rotor will prove to be a tight fit on the crankshaft, and care must be exercised to avoid placing undue strain on the rotor boss or crankshaft. Tighten the extractor bolt until moderate pressure is exerted on the rotor, then apply several sharp blows to the extractor bolt head. The resulting impact will usually jar the rotor free.

5   The alternator stator can be left in position unless it requires specific attention. The crankcase joining screws are arranged around its outside edge and can be removed with the stator in situ. If it is decided to remove the stator, release the two countersunk cross-head screws which retain it and lift it away. The stator is not adjustable in relation to the crankcase, and need not be marked. An impact driver should be used to remove the stator screws without destroying the screw heads.

7.2 Remove the remaining fan cowling screw

7.3 Centre section is secured by three bolts (arrowed)

7.6 Use pliers to remove circlip. Displace pin to free piston

8.2 Fan is held to rotor by three screws

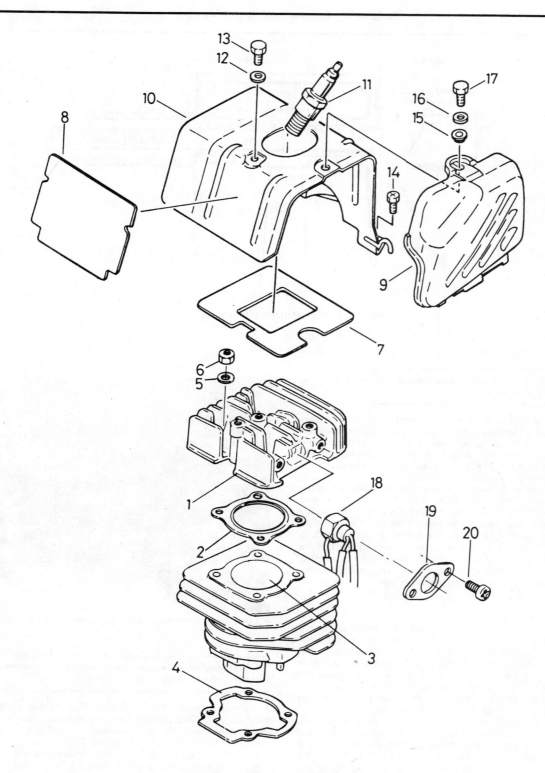

Fig. 1.2 Cylinder head and barrel

1	Cylinder head	8	Rubber flap	15	Collar
2	Cylinder head gasket	9	Plastic cowl	16	Washer
3	Cylinder barrel	10	Cylinder head ducting	17	Bolt
4	Cylinder base gasket	11	Sparking plug	18	BVS valve
5	Plain washer – 4 off	12	Washer	19	Retaining plate
6	Nut – 4 off	13	Bolt	20	Screw – 2 off
7	Baffle	14	Screw – 2 off		

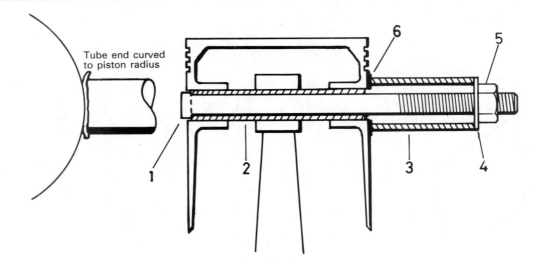

Fig. 1.3 Tool to remove gudgeon pin

1	Extractor bolt	3	Tube	5	Nut
2	Gudgeon pin	4	Washer	6	Rubber washer

9 Dismantling the engine/transmission unit: removing the transmission components

1   Before the chaincase cover is removed it will be necessary to drain the lubricating oil. Place a drain tray under the drain plug at the rear of the casing, remove the plug and leave the unit until the oil has drained off. Note that a certain amount of residual oil will remain in the casing, so have some rags to hand when the cover is removed.

2   Remove the cross-head screws around the periphery of the chaincase cover. The cover will normally lift clear of the inner chaincase, but if it has become stuck to the gasket use a soft-faced mallet to tap around the joint. Take great care not to damage the painted finish of the cover. If essential, it is permissible to ease the joint apart using the prising point on the underside of the cover. Lift the cover away and check whether any thrust washers have stuck to the bosses on the inside of the cover. If so, remove them and place them over their respective shafts.

Two-speed (UK) model

3   Removal of the crankshaft-mounted centrifugal clutch poses similar problems to generator rotor removal, in that it will again be necessary to prevent crankshaft rotation whilst the nut is slackened. This can be achieved by using one of the methods described in the previous Section; if necessary the generator rotor can be refitted to facilitate the use of the holding tool. With the crankshaft immobilised the clutch nut can be slackened and the clutch shoes and boss removed.

4   Unhook the chain tensioner spring from its anchor plate, then slacken the tensioner pivot bolt. The tensioner can be lifted away noting the plain washer fitted on each side of it, and the sleeve upon which it pivots. The clutches and primary drive chain can now be lifted away as an assembly, noting that it will be necessary to displace the drive axle slightly to allow the rear clutch (2nd gear clutch) to clear the 2nd gear driven pinion. If insufficient clearance is available, support the rear of the chain case on blocks and remove the rear wheel by unscrewing the self-locking nut. The splined drive axle can now be pushed through to give the required manoeuvring space.

5   Once the primary drive and clutches have been removed the drive axle can be removed together with its 1st and 2nd gear driven pinions. The assembly can be pushed out of the casing, leaving the bearing and seal in position.

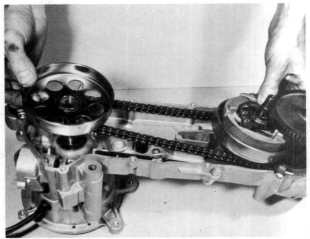

9.4 Dismantle the front clutch, then remove transmission

10 Dismantling the engine/transmission unit: removing the kickstart mechanism

1   The kickstart mechanism is located on the inside of the left-hand engine casing, and need not be disturbed unless it requires specific attention. Start by removing the ratchet gear from the end of the kickstart shaft. This is followed by the large idler gear with which it engages. The idler gear is supported on a shaft to which it is secured by a circlip. Using a pair of pointed-nose pliers, grasp the hooked end of the kickstart return spring and disengage it from its anchor post. Allow the spring to unwind in a controlled manner until it rests against the casing web.

2   Remove the circlip which retains the kickstart quadrant to the splined end of the shaft. Lift the quadrant clear of the shaft, then displace the inner end of the return spring to free it from the shaft. The spring can now be removed. Use a soft-faced mallet to drive the kickstart shaft out of the casing, together with the oil seal, outer circlip and thrust washer. The oil seal should be renewed if there has been any evidence of leakage.

11 Dismantling the engine/transmission unit: separating the crankcase halves

1 Crankshaft separation can only be undertaken after the engine/transmission unit has been removed from the frame and the flywheel generator, primary drive and clutches and the cylinder head, barrel and piston have been removed as described in the preceding Sections. It will also be necessary to remove the reed valve and carburettor adaptor which bridge the crankcase joint. This assembly is retained by four cross-head screws which will probably require the use of an impact driver to remove them. Lift the valve away and place it in a safe place to avoid any chance of damage to the delicate reed valve petals.

2 Using the impact driver, slacken the cross-head screws which secure the crankcase halves. The screws are located in the recessed area of the right-hand crankcase half. With the screws removed the right-hand crankcase half can be pulled off the larger left-hand half. If necessary, tap around the crankcase joint with a soft faced mallet to break the seal. Take great care not to damage any of the weaker areas of the castings. The light alloy castings are rather brittle and can be irreparably damaged by a misplaced blow. If necessary, blows should be concentrated on the large bosses which support the pivot tube and its bearings.

3 As the casing halves separate the pivot tube will be released and can be removed. The crankshaft will remain in one half of the crankcase, and can be dislodged by tapping it through the bearing from the outside. Do not strike the crankshaft end with unnecessary force in view of the risk of distortion. The main bearings can be left undisturbed unless renewal is required. See Section 13 for details.

12 Examination and renovation: general

1 Before examining the parts of the dismantled engine unit for wear it is essential that they should be cleaned thoroughly. Use a paraffin/petrol mix to remove all traces of old oil and sludge that may have accumulated within the engine.

2 Examine the crankcase castings for cracks or other signs of damage. If a crack is discovered, it will require professional repair.

3 Carefully examine each part to determine the extent of wear, checking with the tolerance figures listed in the main text or in the Specifications section of this Chapter. If there is any question of doubt, play safe and renew.

13 Big-end, main and transmission bearings and oil seals: removal and examination

1 Before wear in the big-end can be assessed with any accuracy the crankshaft assembly should be washed in petrol to remove any residual oil. The big-end is checked for wear by arranging the connecting rod in its TDC position. Grasp the connecting rod and pull it firmly upward and then downwards, making sure that any end float, which is intentional, is not mistaken for big-end play. Any discernible up-and-down movement will indicate that the bearing is worn and in need of renewal.

2 The big-end bearing is of the caged needle roller type and under normal circumstances will give good service. If play or roughness is discovered, however, it will be necessary to have the damaged parts renewed. The bearing components are reached by dismantling the pressed-up flywheel assembly, and this must be considered a job for a Yamaha Service Agent. The assembly must be trued up and balanced, a job requiring skills and facilities beyond the reach of most home mechanics. Much of the cost of reconditioning the big-end assembly will have been saved by removing the engine and separating the crankcases.

3 The main bearings should be washed out with petrol and checked for free play. A very small amount of movement is permissible, but severe axial play or any roughness when the bearing is rotated indicates the need for renewal. The bearings can be driven out of their bores once the oil seals have been prised out of position. Note that the seals are likely to be damaged during removal, and should be renewed as a matter of course. Where the bearings prove to be a particularly tight fit in the casing, boiling water can be used to expand the alloy casting, allowing the bearings to be removed with little effort.

4 The remaining bearings and seals can be dealt with in a similar manner, noting that it is good policy to renew the seals as a precautionary measure, even if they appear unscathed during removal. The drive axle bearing is located on its outer face by a large internal circlip.

5 New bearings may be driven into position in casings using a tubular drift against the bearing outer race. Washing the casing with hot water prior to bearing installation will ease the operation. Seals may be fitted using a similar tubular drift. When fitting either type of component ensure that it enters the bore of the housing squarely to prevent tying or jamming.

11.2 Crankcase screws are shown (arrowed)

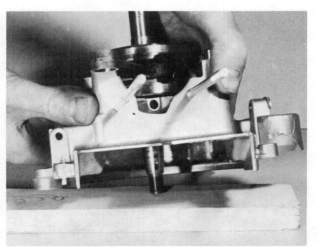

11.3 Crankshaft assembly may be displaced as shown

13.2 Check connecting rod big end for free play

13.3a Prise out and renew worn crankshaft oil seals

13.3b Check and renew main bearings as required

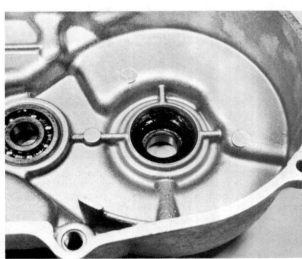

13.4a Stub axle seal should be renewed as a precaution

13.4b Stub axle bearing is retained by a circlip

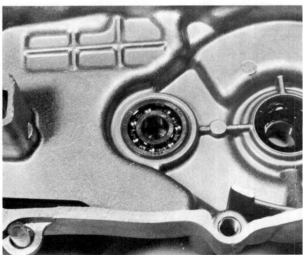

13.4c Check idler shaft bearing for wear

14 Piston and piston rings: examination and renovation

1   Attention to the piston and rings can be overlooked if a rebore is necessary because a new piston and rings will be fitted under these circumstances.

2   If a rebore is not considered necessary, the piston should be examined closely. Reject a piston if it is badly scored or discoloured as the result of the exhaust gases by-passing the rings. Check the gudgeon pin bosses to ensure that they are not enlarged or that the grooves retaining each circlip are not damaged.

3   Remove all carbon from the piston crown using a soft metal or hard wood scraper and taking great care not to scratch the metal surface. Metal polish may be used after the carbon has been removed to obtain a highly polished finish as carbon will adhere much less readily to a polished surface. Examination will show whether the engine has been rebored previously since the amount of overbore is invariably stamped on each piston crown.

4   The grooves in which the piston rings locate can become enlarged in use. Unfortunately, no figure is published for the maximum side clearance. If, however, the clearance exceeds about 0.1 mm (0.004 in) with an unworn ring fitted, ring float may lead to early ring breakage. Before renewing the piston seek the advice of a Yamaha Service Agent.

5   Remove the piston rings by pushing the ends apart with the thumbs whilst gently easing each ring from its groove. Great care is necessary throughout this operation because the rings are brittle and will break easily if overstressed. If the rings are gummed in their grooves, three strips of tin can be used, to ease them free, as shown in the accompanying illustration.

6   Piston ring wear can be checked by inserting the rings one at a time in the cylinder bore from the bottom and pushing them down about 1½ inches with the base of the piston so that they rest squarely in the bore. Make sure that the end gap is away from any of the ports. If the end gap is within the range 0.15 – 0.35 mm (0.006 – 0.014 in) the ring is within the normal specified limits. The service limit is 0.7 mm (0.0276 in).

7   Examine the working surface of each piston ring. If discoloured areas are evident, the ring should be renewed because these areas indicate the blow-by of gas. Check that there is not a build-up of carbon on the back of the ring or in the piston ring groove, which may cause an increase in the radial pressure. A portion of broken ring, the end of which has been ground to a chisel edge, affords the best means of cleaning out the piston ring grooves. If there is the slightest doubt about the condition of the rings they should be renewed. When new rings are fitted without a rebore taking place the bore surface should be honed to remove the glazed bore surface. Failure to do this will prevent correct and speedy running-in of the new components. This operation should be carried out by a motorcycle dealer equipped with a honing device.

8   Check that the piston ring pegs are firmly embedded in each piston ring groove. It is imperative that these retainers should not work loose, otherwise the rings will be free to rotate and there is a danger of the ends being trapped in the ports.

9   It cannot be over-emphasised that the condition of the piston and piston rings is of prime importance because they control the opening and closing of the ports by providing an effective moving seal. A two-stroke engine has only three working parts, of which the piston is one. It follows that the efficiency of the engine is very dependent on the condition of the piston and the parts with which it is closely associated.

10   Check the fit of the gudgeon pin in the piston bosses. Check also the clearance between the gudgeon pin and the small-end bearing. If there is any discernible radial movement, the caged needle roller bearing must be renewed, as should the gudgeon pin if wear is evident on its bearing surface. If the small-end eye itself is oversize the connecting rod must be renewed.

14.6 Piston ring end gap can be checked as shown

14.8 Note locating pegs and piston ring cut-outs

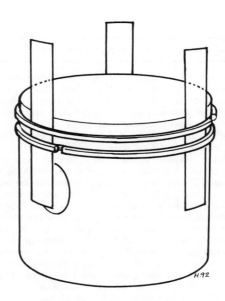

Fig. 1.4 Freeing gummed piston rings

15 Cylinder barrel: examination and renovation

1   The cylinder barrel should be carefully cleaned using a wire brush and petrol to remove any accumulation of grime around the cooling fins. After drying the bore with a clean rag, examine the surface for signs of wear or scoring. If scoring or scratches are in evidence in the bore, the cylinder will need to be rebored and a new piston fitted.

2   A small ridge may be in evidence near to the top of the bore. This marks the extent of travel of the top piston ring, and will probably be more pronounced at one point (the thrust face) than at any other. If this is barely perceptible, and the piston and rings are in good condition, it will probably be safe to use the existing bore. If in any doubt, and in any case if the ridge is marked, the barrel should be taken to a Yamaha Service Agent for checking, together with its piston.

3   For those owners who have the correct equipment the condition of the piston and cylinder barrel may be determined by direct measurement. Measure the diameter of the piston at right-angles to the gudgeon pin line at a point 25 mm (0.975 in) from the bottom of the piston skirt. This figure should be noted and subtracted from the bore diameter measurement (see below) to give the piston to bore clearance. This should be 0.024 – 0.035 mm (0.004 – 0.014 in).

4   The cylinder bore should be measured at three different positions along the length of the cylinder sleeve and then a further three positions at right angles to the first measurements. The manufacturer specifies an ovality limit (the difference between the two sets of measurement described above) of 0.01 mm (0.0004 in) and a taper limit of 0.05 mm (0.002 in). If the above limits are exceeded it will be necessary to have the cylinder barrel rebored and an oversize piston fitted.

5   Clean all carbon deposits from the exhaust ports using a blunt ended scraper. It is important that all the ports should have a clean, smooth appearance because this will have the dual benefit of improving gas flow and making it less easy for carbon to adhere in the future. Finish off with metal polish, to heighten the polishing effect.

6   Do not under any circumstances enlarge or alter the shape of the ports under the mistaken belief that improved performance will result. The size and position of the ports predetermines the characteristics of the engine and unwarranted tampering can produce very adverse effects.

16 Cylinder head: examination and renovation

1   It is unlikely that the cylinder head will require any special attention apart from removing the carbon deposits from the combustion chamber. Finish off with metal polish; the polished surface will help improve gas flow and reduce the tendency of future carbon deposits to adhere so easily.

2   Check that the cooling fins are clean and unobstructed, so that they receive the full air flow.

3   Check the condition of the thread within the sparking plug hole. The thread is easily damaged if the sparking plug is overtightened. If necessary, a damaged thread can be reclaimed by fitting a Helicoil thread insert. Most Yamaha Service Agents have facilities for this type of repair, which is not expensive.

4   If there has been evidence of oil seepage from the cylinder head joint when the machine was in use, check whether the cylinder head is distorted by laying it on a sheet of plate glass. Severe distortion will necessitate renewal of the cylinder head, but if distortion is only slight, the head can be reclaimed by wrapping a sheet of emery paper around the glass and using it as the surface on which to rub down the head with a rotary motion, until it is once again flat. The usual cause of distortion is failure to tighten down the cylinder head nuts evenly, in a diagonal sequence.

17 Transmission system: method of operation

1   The Yamaha Passola models make use of an automatic transmission system which removes the needs for the manual clutch and gearchange controls found on larger machines. In the case of UK models a two-speed arrangement is employed to give better acceleration and hill climbing ability, whilst other European models have a similar system, but having a single speed. Though simple in operation, the systems are more easily maintained if the function of each assembly is understood.

Two-speed models

2   The left-hand end of the crankshaft carries a centrifugal clutch and a drive sprocket assembly (1st clutch) and this automatically connects the engine to the primary drive chain as the engine speed rises above a specified speed (2700 rpm). The clutch is in two main parts; a centre boss which carries the clutch shoes and springs, and an outer drum upon which they bear.

3   At idle speeds, the clutch springs hold the shoes against the boss which is fixed to and rotates with the crankshaft. As the throttle is opened and engine speed rises the clutch shoes are flung outwards against spring tension until they begin to rub on the stationary drum. With further increase in engine speed the pressure against the drum is increased and the latter is turned by the clutch shoes, feeding power to the primary drive chain and causing the machine to move off. Conversely, when the machine slows down a point is reached at which centrifugal force in the hub assembly is less than that exerted by the clutch springs, and the clutch disengages.

4   When the machine moves off initially, power is transmitted via the primary chain to the driven sprocket on the 2nd clutch shaft. A small 1st gear pinion on the same shaft drives its large counterpart on the final drive axle and thence to the rear wheel. When the engine speed reaches 4900 rpm the 2nd clutch engages and the power train is diverted through the second gear pinions. A sprag clutch arrangement in the 1st gear pinion on the final drive axle allows it to freewheel in relation to the axle, thus disconnecting drive through the 1st gear pair.

Single speed models

5   In the case of the single speed machines sold in Sweden and Finland, the front clutch or 1st clutch operates in the same way as described for the two-speed models. The difference lies at the rear of the chaincase, where a single pair of gears transmits drive directly to the final drive axle. Note that the second gear pair, clutch and ratchet are omitted on these models.

18 Centrifugal clutches: examination and renovation

1   Wear in the centrifugal clutches can usually be traced as the cause of most transmission problems. If the clutch linings have become badly worn or glazed there will be a tendency for the clutch to slip, and abnormally high engine speeds will be necessary before the clutch will engage properly. The clutch springs will tend to stretch after high mileages have been covered and this will normally have the opposite effect, the clutch engaging at idle speed, and in severe cases, causing the engine to stall.

2   Deal with each clutch separately to avoid confusion. The front (1st) clutch comprises a base plate with a pivot post at each end to support the clutch shoes. Two tension springs are fitted between the shoes and serve to return the shoes to the centre position when the engine speed drops below a predetermined level. Check the condition of the lining material, noting that the outer end will be noticeably more worn than that nearest to the pivot posts. The nominal lining thickness is 2.3 – 2.4 mm (0.0906 – 0.0945 in), the shoes requiring removal when the material is obviously badly worn. No service limit figures are quoted by the manufacturers, but if clutch slip has

been noticed and the shoes are visibly worn, they should be renewed as a matter of course.

3   Measure the overall free length of each of the clutch springs. In the case of the front clutch, these should be 32 mm (1.260 in). If the springs have become stretched they should be renewed, particularly if the engine has been inclined to stall at tickover or the clutch has tended to engage suddenly when moving off.

4   If it proves necessary to remove the clutch shoes for renewal it will first be necessary to disengage the return springs. Each shoe is now secured to its pivot post by an E-clip and can be slid off once this has been prised off. When reassembling the shoes, check that they pivot freely, and put a trace of high melting point grease on each pivot post.

5   The rear clutch (2nd clutch) is dealt with in a similar fashion, though the shoes are of a slightly more complicated

construction. To dismantle the assembly unhook and remove the clutch springs using a pair of pointed-nose pliers. The shoes are held by a total of four pins to the hub. Prise off the E-clips which retain the pins, displacing them to free the shoe assemblies. The procedure for checking the rear clutch is similar to that described above, noting that the clutch spring free length should be 27 mm (1.063 in). It will be found in practice that worn rear clutch shoes will be indicated by the machine's reluctance to change into 2nd gear, whilst the change will occur prematurely if the clutch springs have become stretched.

6   In the case of both clutches, check the clutch drum for scoring, and renew it where the problem is severe. If the lining surface has become glazed but is otherwise in good condition it is permissible to remove the glazed area using abrasive paper to cure any problems of clutch slip.

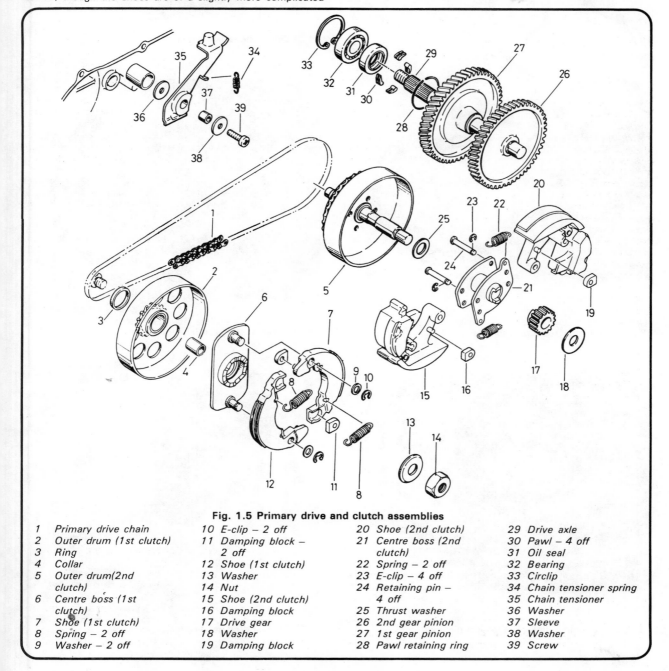

Fig. 1.5 Primary drive and clutch assemblies

1 Primary drive chain	10 E-clip – 2 off	20 Shoe (2nd clutch)	29 Drive axle
2 Outer drum (1st clutch)	11 Damping block – 2 off	21 Centre boss (2nd clutch)	30 Pawl – 4 off
3 Ring	12 Shoe (1st clutch)	22 Spring – 2 off	31 Oil seal
4 Collar	13 Washer	23 E-clip – 4 off	32 Bearing
5 Outer drum(2nd clutch)	14 Nut	24 Retaining pin – 4 off	33 Circlip
6 Centre boss (1st clutch)	15 Shoe (2nd clutch)	25 Thrust washer	34 Chain tensioner spring
7 Shoe (1st clutch)	16 Damping block	26 2nd gear pinion	35 Chain tensioner
8 Spring – 2 off	17 Drive gear	27 1st gear pinion	36 Washer
9 Washer – 2 off	18 Washer	28 Pawl retaining ring	37 Sleeve
	19 Damping block		38 Washer
			39 Screw

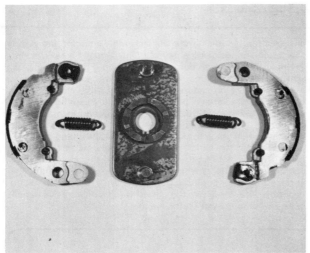

18.2a The front (1st gear) clutch components

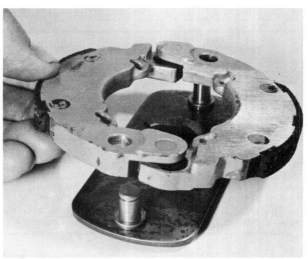

18.2b Clutch shoes locate on pins as shown

18.2c Note damper rubbers in shoe recesses

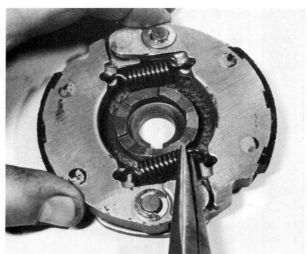

18.4a Fit return springs as shown above

18.4b Do not omit to fit E-clips to pivot pin ends

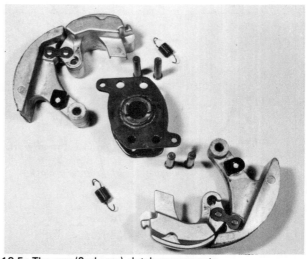

18.5a The rear (2nd gear) clutch components

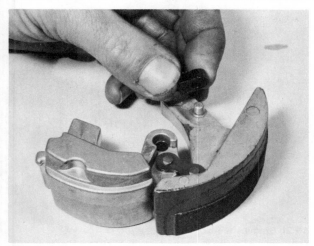

18.5b Damper rubbers are mounted on small pins

18.5c Location pins can be tapped into place as shown

18.5d Fit E-clips to retain pin ends

18.5e Return springs should be fitted as shown

19 Primary drive chain: examination and renovation

1   Engine power is transmitted from the 1st clutch to the final drive gears by way of a single row chain. Unusually, the chain operates under near perfect conditions. It is fully enclosed in the primary chaincase and runs in an oil bath, and is thus kept clean and well lubricated. The centrifugal clutches eliminate many of the shock loadings which chains are usually expected to endure, and this lessens the problem of stretching. A simple spring loaded tensioner arm serves to take up any free play in the chain.

2   Chain condition can be checked with the transmission components in position. It will be found in practice that the chain will last many thousands of miles before renewal becomes necessary. If the chain has stretched to the point where it is in danger of striking the projecting web at the centre of the chain case it should be renewed. Examine the rollers and side plates and renew the chain if these appear worn or damaged. Note that the sprockets must be renewed together with the clutch housings if the teeth appear hooked or chipped.

20 Transmission gears: examination and renovation

1   The large transmission gears at the rear of the chain case are of robust construction and will normally last the life of the machine unless lubrication has been neglected. The condition of the teeth should be examined carefully, especially where gear noise has been evident in use. Look for signs of pitting or chipping on the load faces of the teeth and renew any gears which show signs of severe wear.

2   The small sprag clutch which is located at the centre of the drive axle 1st gear pinion is equally robust and is unlikely to require attention. It can be dismantled for examination after the circlip which locates the gear pinion has been displaced and the pinion slid back to expose the pawls and spring. Any severe wear or damage will be obvious and will require renewal of the affected parts.

21 Kickstart mechanism: examination and renovation

1   The component parts of the kickstart mechanism can be examined for wear or damage after the assembly has been dismantled as described in Section 10. Check the condition of the operating segment and the double idler gear. These are unlikely to show signs of wear under normal conditions, but may require removal if they are damaged. If there has been any tendency for the kickstart ratchet to slip, examine the ratchet teeth. These should have a sharp leading edge and may become rounded in use. The outer part of the ratchet can be renewed as a single component, whilst the inner part is integral with the 1st gear clutch boss and thus must be renewed with it.

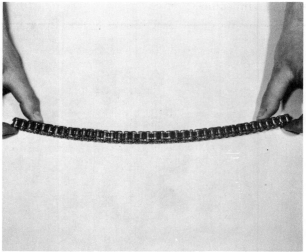
19.2a Badly worn chain will bow much more than this

19.2b Examine teeth of front ...

19.2c ... and rear sprockets for wear or chipping

20.2a Release circlip and thrust washer ...

20.2b ... to allow pinion to be displaced along shaft

20.2c Spring ring around periphery retains pawls

20.2d Pawls should be renewed if worn or damaged

22 Engine reassembly: general

1 Before reassembly of the engine unit is commenced, the various component parts should be cleaned thoroughly and placed on a sheet of clean paper, close to the working area.

2 Make sure all traces of old gaskets have been removed and that the mating surfaces are clean and undamaged. One of the best ways to remove old gasket cement is to apply a rag soaked in methylated spirit. This acts as a solvent and will ensure that the cement is removed without resort to scraping and the consequent risk of damage.

3 Gather together all of the necessary tools and have available an oil can filled with clean engine oil. Make sure that all the new gaskets and oil seals are to hand, also all replacement parts required. Nothing is more frustrating than having to stop in the middle of a reassembly sequence because a vital gasket or replacement has been overlooked.

23 Engine reassembly: joining the crankcase halves

1 Support the left-hand crankcase and chain case casting on the workbench with the crankcase portion of the casting uppermost. Check that the main bearings and oil seals are correctly located in each half and lubricate both with engine oil. Make certain that the gasket faces are clean and free from oil, then apply a thin film of jointing compound to the left-hand gasket face. Place the smaller, right-hand crankcase on wooden blocks and fit the crankshaft assembly through the main bearing, ensuring that it seats squarely. It should be noted that the mainshaft ends are of similar diameter and it is possible to fit the crankshaft the wrong way round unless care is taken. The tapered end should fit through the right-hand main bearing, where it will locate the generator rotor. Fit the locating dowels into their recesses in the casing then offer up the assembled right-hand casing together with the crankshaft. Push the crankcase halves together and check that the gasket faces meet squarely. The retaining screws can now be dropped into position and the joint tightened down. Use an impact driver to secure the screws in a diagonal sequence. Before moving on to other reassembly operations, check that the crankshaft can be rotated smoothly and easily.

24 Engine reassembly: refitting the flywheel generator

1 Fit the Woodruff key into the recessed portion of the tapered crankshaft end, tapping it firmly into place. Thread the leads from the generator stator coils through the hole in the rear of the generator housing and then draw them through until the tapered end of the grommet enters the hole. The grommet should be eased into position so that it seals the hole. Position the generator stator against the rear wall of the housing and insert and tighten the retaining screws. It will be noted that the countersunk retaining screws hold the stator in the correct position, there being no provision for ignition timing adjustment.

2 Lower the rotor into position over the crankshaft end, ensuring that the key engages correctly in the keyway. Fit the plain and spring washers followed by the retaining nut. Lock the crankshaft using whichever method was employed during removal. Using a torque wrench, tighten the securing nut to 4.3 kgf m (31.1 lbf ft).

23.1a Grease oil seal lips prior to assembly

23.1b Apply non-hardening sealant to crankcase joint

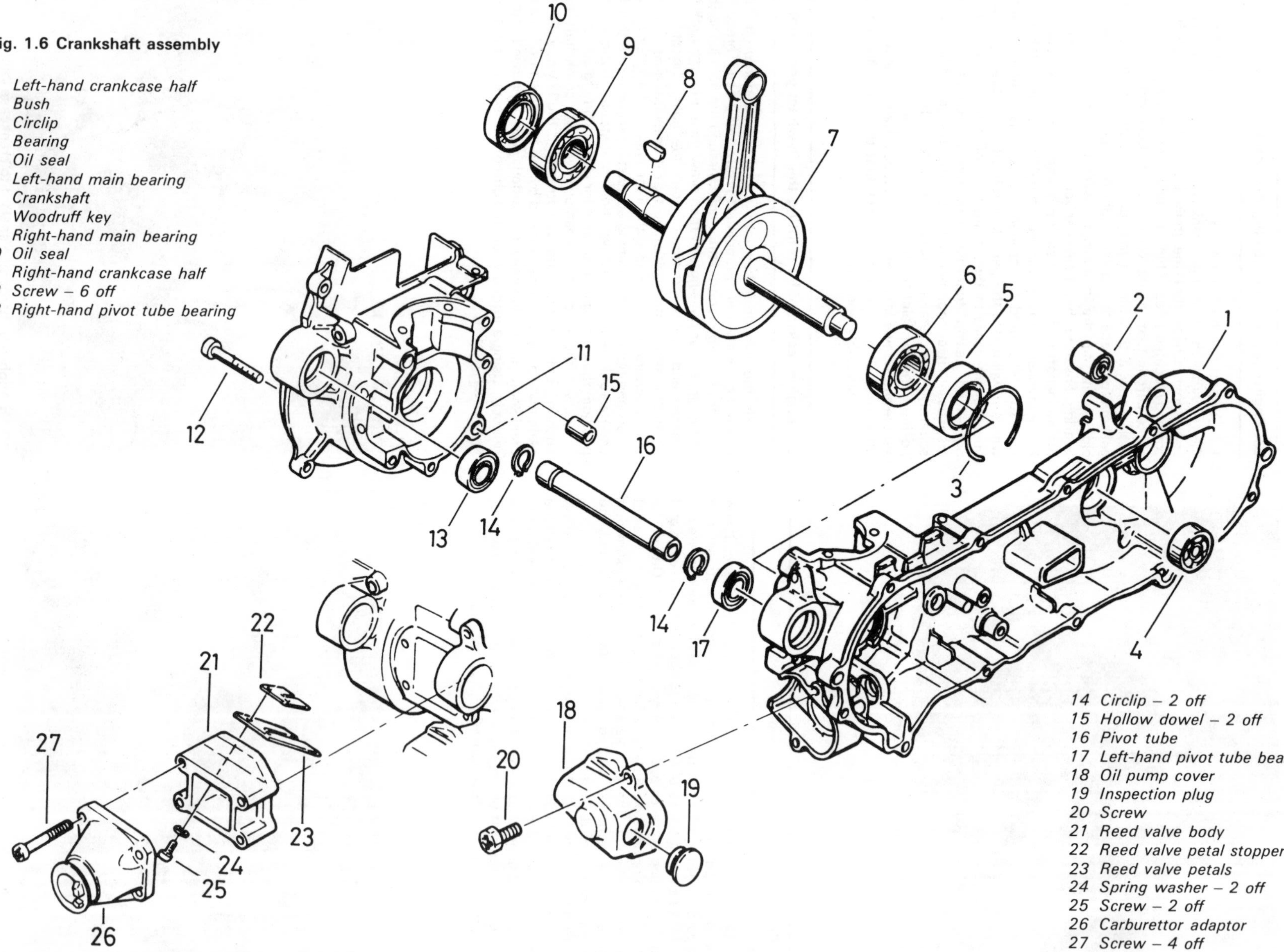

Fig. 1.6 Crankshaft assembly

1 Left-hand crankcase half
2 Bush
3 Circlip
4 Bearing
5 Oil seal
6 Left-hand main bearing
7 Crankshaft
8 Woodruff key
9 Right-hand main bearing
10 Oil seal
11 Right-hand crankcase half
12 Screw – 6 off
13 Right-hand pivot tube bearing

14 Circlip – 2 off
15 Hollow dowel – 2 off
16 Pivot tube
17 Left-hand pivot tube bearing
18 Oil pump cover
19 Inspection plug
20 Screw
21 Reed valve body
22 Reed valve petal stopper
23 Reed valve petals
24 Spring washer – 2 off
25 Screw – 2 off
26 Carburettor adaptor
27 Screw – 4 off

23.1c Crankshaft should be fitted as shown ...

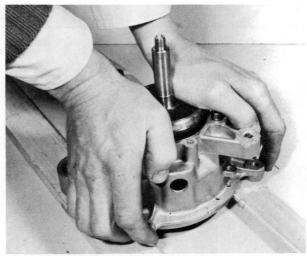

23.1d ... and pushed firmly into bearing

23.1e Fit locating dowels into casing recesses ...

23.1f ... then offer up right-hand crankcase half

23.1g Fit and tighten the crankcase screws

24.1a Fit generator stator (where it was removed)

24.1b Stator is secured by countersunk screws

24.2a Place rotor over crankshaft end ...

24.2b ... and fit the locking washer and nut

24.2c Tighten the nut to the recommended torque setting

25 Engine reassembly: refitting the transmission components

1   Slide the oil pump drive gear over the crankshaft end, noting that the extended metal boss should face inwards. Ensure that the keyway is correctly aligned so that it engages with the key in the crankshaft end. It may prove necessary to rotate the crankshaft as the gear engages with the pump pinion.
2   Slide the assembled final drive axle through the bearing, having lubricated the oil seal lip with grease. Do not fit the rear wheel at this stage because a certain amount of manoeuvring will be necessary to allow the rear clutch assembly to be fitted. Assemble the rear (2nd gear) clutch and housing, noting that a thrust washer is fitted between the two. Lay out the front clutch housing and the rear clutch assembly and fit the primary drive chain around the front and rear sprockets. The entire assembly can be lowered into position, noting that a thin spacer is fitted between the oil pump drive gear and the front clutch, together with the bush or collar upon which the clutch housing turns.

3   As the assembly is offered up it will be necessary to withdraw the final drive axle so that the rear clutch can be positioned between the 1st and 2nd speed driven gears. Once it is in position, fit the small Woodruff key into the slot in the crankshaft end. The front clutch can now be lowered into position and the locking washer and nut fitted, the former with its convex face outwards. Tighten the securing nut to 2.5 – 3.5 kgf m (18.1 – 25.3 lbf ft).
4   If it has been removed in the course of overhaul, place the chain guide in position at the bottom of the chaincase, securing it by fitting the tensioner spring anchor plate and its single retaining screw. Place the tubular rubber spacer over the cast projection at the centre of the chaincase. Assemble the tensioner pivot screw noting that a small bush is fitted around the screw and that a large plain washer is positioned on each side of the tensioner arm. Place the assembly in the casing and tighten the pivot screw. Fit the small tension spring between the tensioner arm and the casing anchor point. Place the 2nd speed gear, shim and plain washer as shown in the accompanying photographs.

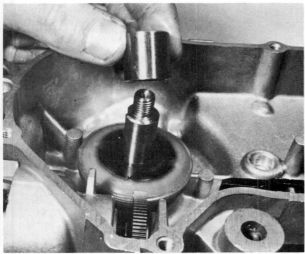

25.1a Slide oil pump gear and clutch bush into place

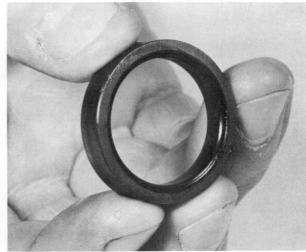

25.1b Note special sealed spacer ...

25.1c ... which is fitted as shown

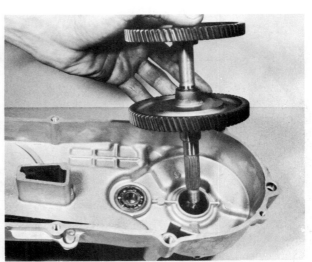

25.2a Assemble and fit the stub axle assembly

25.2b Note thrust washer between housing and clutch

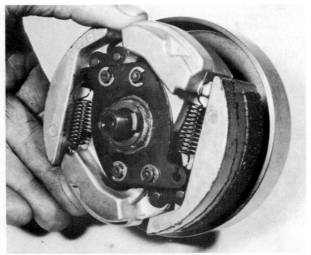

25.2c Assemble clutch and fit primary drive chain

25.2d Transmission assembly can be installed as shown

25.3a Fit small square-section key into crankshaft slot

25.3b Place front (1st speed) clutch into housing

25.3c Fit locking washer, convex side outwards

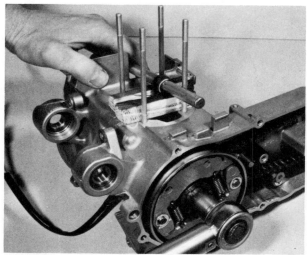

25.3d Lock crankshaft and secure clutch nut

25.4a Fit chain guide as shown (where it was removed) ...

25.4b ... and secure with plate and screw

25.4c Assemble the chain tensioner and pivot ...

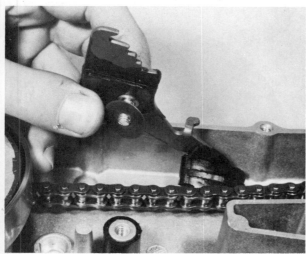

25.4d ... and install in casing

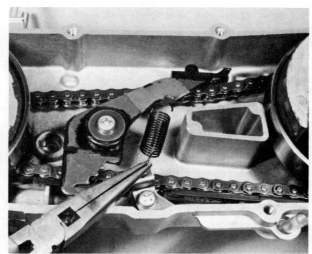

25.4e Fit the tensioner spring as shown

25.4f Place gear over shaft, noting engagement dogs

25.4g Fit the small shim ...

25.4h ... and the plain washer

26.1a Pack crankcase mouth with rag and fit small-end bearing

26 Engine reassembly: refitting the piston

1   Before the piston is refitted, cover the crankcase opening with rag to obviate any risk of a displaced circlip entering the crankcase. The piston has an arrow stamped on the crown which must point down towards the exhaust port when fitted. Note that on this engine unit the exhaust port is to the *rear* of the barrel.

2   If the gudgeon pin is a tight fit in the piston boss, the piston can be warmed with warm water to effect the necessary temporary expansion. Oil the gudgeon pin, the small-end bearing and piston bosses before the gudgeon pin is inserted, then fit the circlips, making sure that they are engaged fully with their retaining grooves. A good fit is essential, since a displaced circlip will cause extensive engine damage. Always fit new circlips, NEVER re-use the old ones.

3   Check that the piston rings are fitted correctly, with their ends either side of the ring pegs, Note that the rings cannot engage on the locating pegs unless they are fitted the right way up. The peg and ring cut-outs are off-set in relation to the ring groove to prevent this.

26.1b Arrow mark on piston crown must face exhaust port

27 Engine reassembly: refitting the cylinder barrel and cylinder head

1   Place a new cylinder base gasket over the cylinder barrel spigot and lubricate the cylinder bore with clean engine oil. Arrange the piston so that it is at top dead centre (TDC) and supported by two wooden blocks placed across the crankcase mouth. Lower the cylinder barrel over the piston crown. The rings can now be squeezed one at a time until the cylinder barrel will slide over them, checking to ensure that the ends are still each side of the ring peg. Great care is necessary during this operation, since the rings are brittle and very easily broken.

2   When the rings have engaged fully with the cylinder bore withdraw the rag packing from the crankcase mouth and slide the cylinder barrel down so that it seats on the new base gasket. No gasket cement should be used either with or instead of the base gasket.

3   Fit a new cylinder head gasket over the holding studs. The gasket is of the all metal type and cannot be re-used because the sealing rib will have become compressed. No gasket cement should be used on this joint. Lower the cylinder head into position and place the washers and nuts on the holding down studs. The nuts should be fitted finger tight, and then secured by turning them by about $\frac{1}{4}$ turn at a time in a diagonal sequence. This will obviate any risk of distortion. The nuts should be tightened to a torque of 0.8 – 1.2 kgf m (5.69 – 8.68 lbf ft).

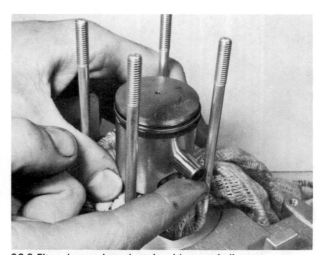

26.2 Fit gudgeon pin and retain with **new** circlips

27.1a Place new gasket on cylinder barrel base

27.1b Feed rings into barrel mouth as shown

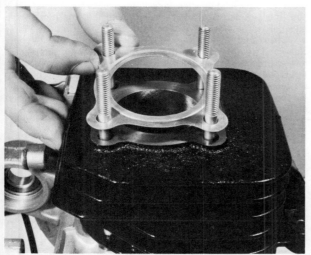

27.3a Place new cylinder head gasket over studs

27.3b Lower the cylinder head into position

27.3c Fit the cylinder head nuts and tighten correctly

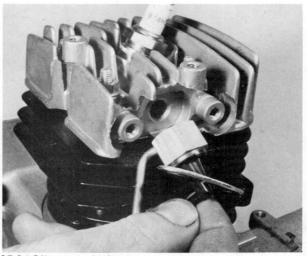

27.3d Offer up the BVS valve ...

27.3e ... and retain with its two screws

28 Engine reassembly: fitting the kickstart mechanism and chaincase cover

1   Fit the locating circlip to the kickstart shaft, then slide the thrust washer up against the inner face of the circlip. Slide the shaft into the casing until the washer and circlip butt against the

recessed bore. The oil seal can be fitted next, noting that a new seal should be used unless it is known that the old item is in good condition. In either case, grease the seal lip prior to installation. Slide the seal over the end of the shaft taking great care not to damage the delicate seal lip on the splines. A tubular drift will be required to fit the seal, a suitably sized socket being ideal for this.

2   Moving to the inside of the casing, drop the kickstart return spring over the shaft end, noting that the inner tang of the spring should face away from the casing. The outer tang should be allowed to rest against the cast lug which normally holds the friction clip. Offer up the toothed quadrant, engaging the inner tang of the spring in the cut-out in the quadrant. The quadrant should be turned against spring pressure through approximately 90° until its flat face lies parallel to the centreline of the casing (see photographs). The quadrant can now be pushed home until it engages with the splines on the shaft.

3   Grasp the free end of the spring with a pair of pointed-nose pliers and turn it until it can be hooked around the anchor post. The quadrant must now be secured by fitting the circlip which retains it with the shaft. Place the double idler gear over the support pin and engage the smaller gear with the quadrant teeth. Fit the E-clip which retains it, then place the ratchet block over the kickstart shaft end, making sure that the friction clip engages in the slot provided in the casing.

4   Check that the jointing faces of the chaincase and cover are clean and free from oil. Fit the two locating dowels and place a new gasket in position. Fit the conical spring washer and plain thrust washer to the end of the rear clutch shaft, then offer up the cover. Fit and tighten the securing screws around the perimeter of the cover. Before moving on, fit the kickstart lever and check that the kickstart mechanism operates correctly.

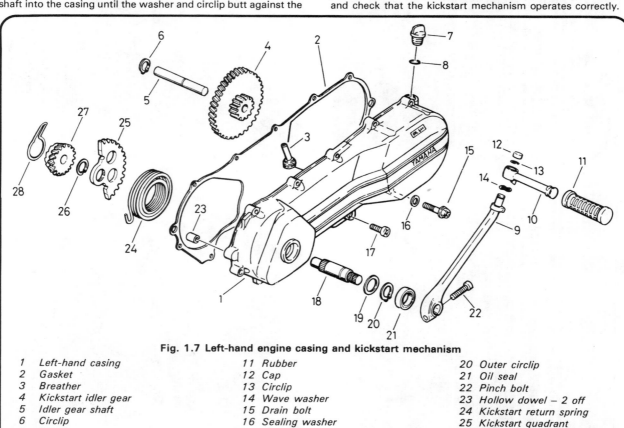

Fig. 1.7 Left-hand engine casing and kickstart mechanism

1 Left-hand casing	11 Rubber	20 Outer circlip
2 Gasket	12 Cap	21 Oil seal
3 Breather	13 Circlip	22 Pinch bolt
4 Kickstart idler gear	14 Wave washer	23 Hollow dowel – 2 off
5 Idler gear shaft	15 Drain bolt	24 Kickstart return spring
6 Circlip	16 Sealing washer	25 Kickstart quadrant
7 Filler plug	17 Screw – 10 off	26 Circlip
8 O-ring	18 Kickstart shaft	27 Ratchet gear
9 Kickstart lever	19 Thrust washer	28 Kick clip
10 Lever end		

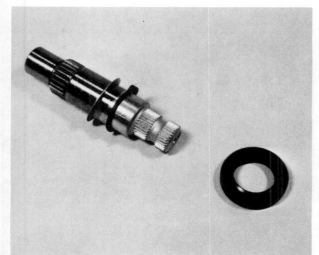

28.1a Fit circlip and washer to the kickstart shaft

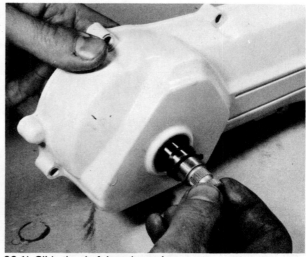

28.1b Slide the shaft into the casing ...

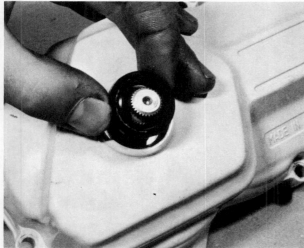

28.1c ... followed by the oil seal

28.1d A large socket can be used to press seal into place

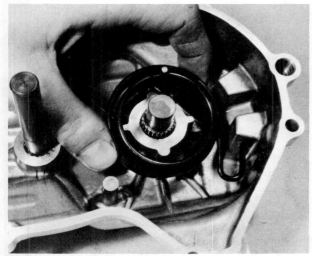

28.2a Fit the kickstart return spring as shown ...

28.2b ... followed by the quadrant

28.3a Use pliers to hook spring end over projection

28.3b Secure the quadrant with a circlip

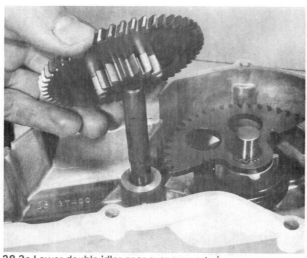
28.3c Lower double idler gear over support pin ...

28.3d ... and return it with an E-clip

28.3e Fit ratchet block noting slot for friction clip (arrowed)

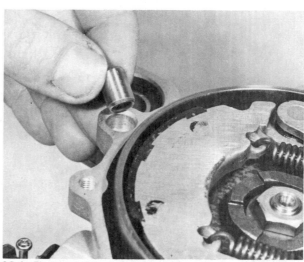
28.4a Fit dowels into casing recesses ...

28.4b ... and place a new gasket into position

28.4c Fit the outer cover and securing screws

29 Engine reassembly: fitting the reed valve, intake adaptor and swinging arm pivot sleeve

1   Check that the mating surface on the crankcase is clean and check the O-ring which seals the reed valve case to the crankcase. If it appears compressed or damaged it should be renewed. Assemble the reed valve unit and the intake adaptor, dropping the mounting screws into position to locate the two components. Offer up the assembly and fit the retaining screws, tightening them evenly in a diagonal sequence to prevent distortion of the reed valve case.

2   A tubular steel sleeve is supported between the two swinging arm pivot bearings and should be fitted as follows. Slide the sleeve through the centre of one of the bearings until it lies about half way from its normal position. Fit one of the two locating circlips well inboard of the retaining groove, then fit the remaining clip in the groove. Slide the sleeve fully home so that the second clip locates against the bearing, then fit the first circlip to the remaining locating groove. (See photographs).

29.1a Assemble the reed valve unit and adaptor ...

30 Engine reassembly: fitting the fan and engine cooling shrouds

1   Offer up the plastic cooling fan and fit the three screws which secure it to the generator rotor. Place the metal centre section of the cooling shroud over the cylinder head and barrel, noting that the synthetic rubber absorber pad should be placed between it and the cylinder head, where applicable. This latter item is shown in the relevant factory information, but was not fitted on the machine featured in the accompanying photographs. A second rubber section is trapped between the front of the centre section and the cooling fins and acts as a deflector.

2   Secure the centre section with two screws at its rear edge and the single bolt and plain washer which screws into the cylinder head. Fit the smaller plastic side cowl, ensuring that its lower edge engages with the cast lugs on the crankcase. Fit the headed spacer, plain washer and bolt which retains it and the left-hand side of the centre section to the cylinder head.

3   Offer up the larger right-hand cowl and secure it with the upper front retaining screw, noting that a cable clip should be fitted to the screw head first. The remaining two fixing screws also retain the exhaust heat shield, and should be left off at this stage.

29.1b ... and fit as shown

29.2a Slide pivot sleeve through bearing ...

29.2b ... position circlips as shown ...

29.2c ... then slide clips back into location grooves

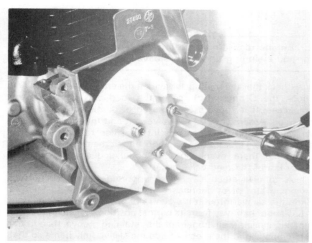
30.1 Fan is secured by three screws

31 Engine reassembly: fitting the stand, exhaust system and rear wheel

1   Invert the engine/transmission unit on the workbench to gain access to the exhaust port area. Check that the port and exhaust pipe flange are both clean and dry, and fit a new sealing ring. To facilitate assembly it is worth making sure that the sealing ring is firmly attached to the exhaust pipe flange, and to this end it can be located with one or two spots of glue. One of the popular iso-cyanoacrylate 'super glues' is both quick and convenient, but should be used very sparingly and observing the manufacturer's safety precautions.

2   Offer up the exhaust system, guiding the slotted flange around the two manifold bolts. Fit the two silencer mounting bolts finger-tight, then tighten the flange bolts to 1.0 kgf m (7.2 lbf ft). The silencer mounting bolts can now be tightened to 1.8 kgf m (13.0 lbf ft).

3   It is advisable to fit the stand whilst the engine unit is inverted. The stand and its return spring are fitted as an assembly, there being no practicable alternative method. How-

ever the operation is approached it is not easy, and it is almost essential to have a second pair of hands to hold the unit steady and push the pivot pin into position. Fit the return spring to the casing lug, and hook the free end of the anchor pin on the stand. Push the pivot pin through the stand and into the casting bore at the end opposite the spring. With an assistant holding the engine unit and ready to tap the pivot pin through, pull the stand against spring tension until it aligns. This stage will probably take several attempts. Once the pin has been pushed through, fit the plain washer and split pin.

4   Support the engine/transmission unit on the work bench, using the centre stand and blocks beneath the rear of the chaincase. If it was removed for any reason, the rear brake backplate assembly should be refitted and the three mounting bolts tightened to 1.8 kgf m (13.0 lbf ft). Do not omit to bend up the locking tabs to secure the bolts. Slide the plain thrust washer over the projecting end of the drive axle, then offer up the rear wheel. Fit the plain washer and nut, tightening the latter to 6.0 kgf m (43.4 lbf ft) and securing it using a new split pin. The engine/transmission assembly will now rest quite securely, supported by the rear wheel and the centre stand.

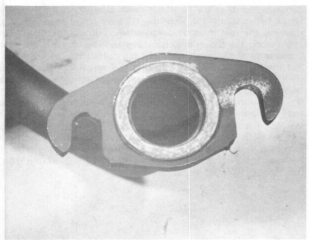

31.1 Exhaust port seal should be stuck to flange

31.2 Flange is located at port as shown

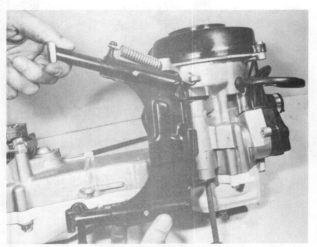

31.3a Position the stand and fit pivot pin ...

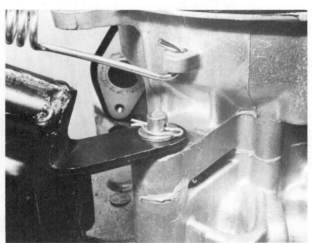

31.3b ... retaining it with a washer and R-pin

32 Installing the engine/transmission unit and final assembly

1   It is convenient to join the engine/transmission unit and the chassis at this stage. In view of the fact that the frame assembly must be fitted into place above the engine unit, an assistant must be considered essential if damage to the paintwork or owner is to be avoided. Before starting work make sure that there is adequate space to the front of the engine/transmission unit to allow the frame to be manoeuvred back and above it.

2   Support the frame to the rear of the seat and lift it into position above the engine unit. An assistant should be on hand to align the engine mounting sleeve between the ends of the frame-mounted support bracket. Once in line the pivot bolt can be inserted and the rear suspension mounting bolt fitted, thus supporting the rear of the frame. The pivot bolt should be tightened to 4.5 kgf m (32.5 lbf ft). The upper suspension mounting should be tightened to 2.3 kgf m (16.6 lbf ft) and the lower mounting to 1.8 kgf m (13.0 lbf ft).

3   Offer up the carburettor together with the vacuum fuel tap and the interconnecting pipes. The carburettor should be fitted to the inlet adaptor and the securing clamp tightened. Note that a slot in the adaptor engages with a tang on the carburettor

giving approximate alignment, but care should be taken to make sure that the instrument is mounted vertically to ensure that the correct fuel level is maintained in the float bowl.

4   The vacuum fuel tap is secured to its mounting bracket by two screws. Once in position refit the pipe from the fuel tank, then connect the various fuel, breather and vacuum hoses between the carburettor, fuel tap and the BVS valve on the cylinder head. It is vital that these are connected properly, and reference should be made to Fig. 1.1 which illustrates this.

5   Refit the long oil feed pipe between the oil tank and the pump, then fill the tank with two-stroke oil. It is necessary to bleed the lubrication system to remove any air bubbles which might otherwise starve the engine of lubrication. To this end a bleed screw is fitted to the pump. This screw is fitted to a tubular extension of the pump body casting and is located at the uppermost edge of the pump. It can be identified by its sealing washer. It should be noted that the bleeding operation is inclined to be messy, and some provision must be made to catch any waste oil.

6   Remove the bleed screw and watch the oil as it emerges from the bleed hole. There will be some delay while the air in the feed pipe is displaced after which a mixture of oil and air bubbles will be produced. The screw can be refitted once the emerging oil is free of air bubbles. To complete the bleeding

operation it is essential that the small bore delivery pipe from the pump to the inlet tract is primed with oil. It should be noted that the amount of oil injected is very small, and if the pipe were left empty there would be a considerable delay (up to 25 minutes), before oil reached the engine. To preclude engine seizure fill the pipe with two-stroke oil using a normal trigger-operated oil can, then refit the pipe, remembering to slide the tubular steel clip into place to retain it.

7   Reconnect the oil pump operating cable to the pump pulley, and check that the cable follows a smooth U-shaped path to the splitter box below the floor boards (see Fig. 1.8). Check the pump settings as described in Section 33, noting that this must be done after the engine has been started. To this end, leave the pump cover off until the pump settings have been checked.

8   Refit the air cleaner assembly to the frame, and connect the flexible trunking between it and the carburettor. Reconnect the

generator leads at the multi-pin connector and at the adjacent single bullet connector. Refit the HT lead at the sparking plug, then clip the rear mudguard into position. Route the rear brake cable along the top of the chaincase and connect it at the rear brake arm, and clamp the end of the outer cable in its recess. Set the rear brake adjuster so that the wheel is free to rotate with the brake off, but ensure that it operates as soon as the lever is operated.

9   Fit the exhaust heat shield noting the long spacer on the front mounting screw. Do not omit to fit the asbestos heat insulation washer, spacer and grommet on the rear retaining screw. Refit and connect the battery, and check that the electrical system functions normally. Remove the filler plug at the rear of the chaincase and add 650 cc (22.9/22.0 Imp/US fl oz) of SAE 10W/30 motor oil.

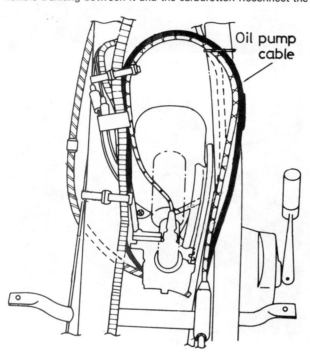

Fig. 1.8 Oil pump operating cable routing

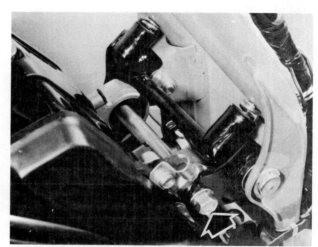

32.2 Fit and tighten the engine pivot bolt

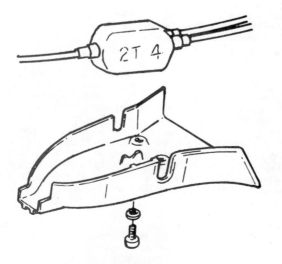

Fig. 1.9 Throttle cable and oil pump cable splitter box

32.3 Carburettor should be fitted inside mounting stub

32.4 Note hose connections when fitting vacuum fuel tap

32.6 Prime oil delivery pipe using oil can (arrowed)

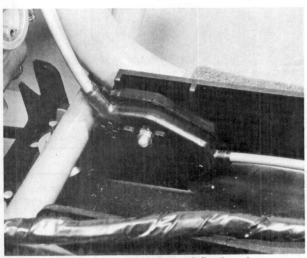
32.7 Note cable splitter location beneath floorboard

32.8a Assemble the air cleaner case and trunking

32.8b Note routing of rear brake cable through guide

32.8c Refit sparking plug and high tension lead

33 Starting and running the rebuilt engine

1　The rebuilt unit should be started and checked over at this stage, before the various panels and covers are refitted. Make a final examination of the machine to check that the various cables, pipe and electrical leads are connected, then switch the ignition on and attempt to start the engine. It will be necessary to spin the engine over for some time so that the fuel tap operates and fills the carburettor float bowl. When the engine starts there will be an excessive amount of smoke for a few minutes until the oil used during assembly has burnt off. This should gradually subside as the engine warms up.

2　Once the engine is idling satisfactorily, check the alignment of the oil pump as follows. Gradually open the throttle twistgrip until the free play in the cable has just been taken up. Check that at this point the cross-headed pin on the pump barrel coincides with the raised alignment marks on the pump pulley. If necessary, adjustment can be made by means of the in-line adjuster in the pump cable. Once set, the pump cover can be refitted and the panels and cowls refitted in the reverse of the dismantling sequence. The machine can now be road tested.

3　Remember that a good seal between the piston and the cylinder barrel is essential for the correct function of the engine. A rebored two-stroke engine will require more carefully running-in, over a longer period, than its four-stroke counterpart. There is a far greater risk of engine seizure during the first hundred miles if the engine is permitted to work hard.

4　Do not tamper with the exhaust system or use a holed or damaged silencer. Unwarranted changes in the exhaust system will have a very marked effect on engine performance, in-variably for the worse. The same advice applies to dispensing with the air cleaner.

5　Do not on any account add extra oil to the petrol under the mistaken belief that a little extra oil will improve the engine lubrication. Apart from creating excess smoke, the addition of oil will make the mixture much weaker, with the consequent risk of overheating and engine seizure.

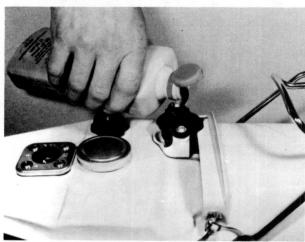

33.1 Check that oil tank is full before starting engine

34 Fault diagnosis: engine

Symptom	Cause	Remedy
Engine will not start	Defective sparking plug	Remove plug and lay it on cylinder head Check whether spark occurs when engine is kicked over
	Fuel tank empty	Refill
Engine runs unevenly	Ignition and/or fuel system fault	Check as though engine will not start
	Blowing cylinder head joint	Oil leak should provide evidence. Check for warpage
	Choked silencer	Remove and clean
Lack of power	Fault in fuel system	Check system
	Choked silencer	See above
White smoke from exhaust	Engine needs rebore	Rebore and fit oversize piston
	Tank contains two-stroke petroil	Drain and refill with straight petrol
Engine overheats	Pre-ignition and/or weak mixture	Check carburettor settings also grade of plug fitted

35 Fault diagnosis: transmission

Symptom	Cause	Remedy
Engine will not turn over when kickstart lever operated	Kickstart mechanism worn or damaged	Dismantle and overhaul
Engine runs normally but road speed low	Transmission will not shift into second gear	Check second (rear) clutch for wear or jamming
Engine stalls at idle speed	First clutch jammed or spring worn or broken	Dismantle and overhaul
Engine speed rises but machine fails to move or moves very slowly	First clutch slipping or jammed	Dismantle and overhaul

Chapter 2 Fuel system and lubrication

For information and revisions to later models, see Chapter 7

Contents

Specifications

	UK models	Other models
Fuel tank		
Capacity	5.28 Imp pints(3.0 litres)	
Carburettor		
Make	Teikei	Teikei
Type	Y12P	Y8P
ID mark	2T403	3W900
Main jet	94	74
Air jet	1.5	1.5
Jet needle	3S42-3	3S60-2
Needle position	5	5
Needle jet	2.100	2.100
Cutaway	2.5	2.5
Pilot jet	40	40
Air screw (turns out)	$1\frac{1}{2}$	$1\frac{1}{2}$
Starter jet	42	42
Fuel level	20 ± 1 mm (0.7874 ± 0.0394 in)	
Float height	25 ± 1 mm (0.9843 ± 0.0394 in)	
Engine idle speed	1700 rpm	
Lubrication system		
Type	Pump fed from separate oil tank	
Make	Yamaha Autolube	
Pump colour code	Green	
Minimum stroke	0.30 - 0.35 mm (0.0118 - 0.0138 in)	
Maximum stroke	1.20 - 1.35 mm (0.0472 - 0.0531 in)	
Minimum output per 200 strokes	0.28 - 0.33 cc (0.0017 - 0.0201 cu in)	
Maximum output per 200 strokes	1.15 - 1.29 cc (0.0702 - 0.0787 cu in)	

1 General description

The fuel system is unusually sophisticated for a small capacity two-stroke machine, featuring a number of rather complex devices which serve to remove a number of minor manual controls. The carburettor is of the normal slide type but features a diaphragm operated cold start plunger. This is opened by engine vacuum when the engine is cold, its action being controlled by a bimetallic valve in the cylinder head. This latter component is known as a BVS valve (Bimetal vacuum switching valve).

Fuel is fed to the carburettor by a fully automatic vacuum fuel tap mounted on the frame. This too is controlled by engine vacuum, and is interconnected with the BVS valve and cold start (automatic choke) system, providing a vacuum source for these components. These systems are quite straightforward once the function of each is understood, and reference should be made to the sections describing their function elsewhere in this Chapter.

The fuel/air mixture is admitted to the engine via a reed valve assembly which allows more accurate timing of the mixture than conventional piston porting alone. The valve is entirely automatic in operation, opening and closing according to changes in pressure inside the crankcase.

Lubrication of the engine unit is by pump, a precisely metered amount of two-stroke oil being injected via a small nozzle on the carburettor. The amount of oil is varied according to the throttle opening, the pump stroke being controlled by a cable connected to the throttle twistgrip.

The Passola features a unique method of cold starting which operates as follows. When the engine is cold, a spring beneath the cold start plunger opens the system ready for starting. When the kickstart lever is depressed the system provides an extremely rich starting mixture, and this continues to be supplied to the engine until it warms up to its normal operating temperature. During this period the BVS valve on the cylinder head blocks the port which leads to the area below the cold start diaphragm.

As the engine reaches normal operating temperature the bimetal strip in the BVS valve opens the cold start port allowing engine vacuum to be applied to the area beneath the cold start diaphragm. The reduced pressure allows the spring to be overcome by atmospheric pressure, and the cold start system is turned off. If the engine is stopped, a slight vacuum is maintained thus keeping the cold start system off until the BVS valve senses that the engine has cooled sufficiently to require a rich starting mixture. At this point atmospheric pressure is admitted to the pipe between the BVS valve and the diaphragm and the spring pushes the cold start plunger back to the 'On' position.

The pipe connections for the auto choke system are as follows. The pipe which connects the auto choke diaphragm to the BVS valve is identified by a conntinuous row of Cs printed along its length. The two remaining pipes from the BVS valve are vacuum feeds and are marked A and B. These are connected to stubs on the inner edge of the vacuum fuel tap. The three pipes connected to the BVS valve are charcoal grey in colour, and in the case of the machine featured in this manual were identified by a continuous row of coding letters (A, B and C). It would appear that a different coding system may have been featured on earlier versions, in which the A and C pipes were grey and the B pipe grey with a white ring at the end. Whichever system is used, check that it corresponds with the pipe connection diagram (Fig. 2.1).

2   Fuel tank: removal and refitting

1   To gain access to the fuel tank it will be necessary to remove the surrounding bodywork, namely the rear cowl and luggage rack, the side panels and the front cowl. The procedure for removing these components is described in Chapter 1, Section 3. Once these have been removed it is relatively easy to reach the tank mountings.

2   Lift the seat, and remove it by releasing the nut which retains its pivot pin. The pin can be displaced to allow the seat to be lifted away. Obtain a clean *metal* container of at least $\frac{1}{2}$ gallon (3.0 litre) capacity into which the petrol can be drained. Remove the tank to tap feed pipe at the frame-mounted vacuum fuel tap and allow the fuel to drain.

3   The tank is secured at four points by nuts and studs. Two of these secure the tank to the cross brace between the frame tubes, whilst two additional mountings locate the rear edge of the tank to lugs on the frame. Once these have been freed, the tank can be lifted away. Reassembly is a straightforward reversal of the removal sequence.

3   Petrol tank: flushing

1   The fuel tank may need flushing out occasionally to remove any accumulated debris which inevitably builds up over the years. This is especially true if water has contaminated the fuel, as this can cause persistent and annoying running problems as it gets drawn into the carburettor.

2   Flushing is best done by first removing the tank, as detailed in the preceeding Section, and then draining the tank of any contaminated fuel. Any debris or water may now be cleaned out by flushing the tank with clean petrol. Note that this operation must be undertaken outdoors and away from naked flames or lights, otherwise serious personal injury may result from the ignition of the petrol vapour.

4   Fuel and vacuum pipes: examination and renovation

1   The condition of the fuel and vacuum pipes connected to the fuel tap should be checked periodically. The synthetic rubber pipes are quite resistant to deterioration, but may eventually develop leaks where they push over their respective stubs. This can be corrected by disconnecting the pipe and slicing off the worn end. For obvious reasons this cannot be repeated many times before renewal becomes necessary.

2   Always obtain replacement pipes of the correct type, especially where identification marks are present. Replacement pipes of different materials should be avoided, and natural rubber tubing must be avoided at all costs. This latter material is attacked by fuel and will disintegrate internally blocking the carburettor jets with a thick rubbery sludge.

5   Carburettor: removal and replacement

1   The carburettor is located at the front of the engine/transmission unit, and can be reached once the front cowl has been removed. The cowl can be removed by releasing the two front side panel screws and the single central screw. Note that the cowl extends from the area immediately below the seat to the footboard, the two sections being riveted together to form a single panel.

2   Pull off the moulded trunking which connects the carburettor intake to the air cleaner casing. The trunking is secured by wire spring retainers at either end and is easily removed. Before the carburettor can be lifted away it will be necessary to disconnect the various pipes which run between it and the vacuum fuel tap, BVS valve and the oil pump. It is essential that these are not confused during reassembly, so study the position of each one, comparing it with the routing diagram (Fig. 2.1) before any attempt is made to release them.

3   Start by pulling off the vacuum pipe from the top of the diaphragm. This is a charcoal grey pipe which runs to the C outlet of the BVS valve and is normally marked with a line of Cs along its length. From the left-hand side of the carburettor and working from front to back remove the breather pipe, fuel pipe and the vacuum take-off pipe. Finally, remove the small diameter oil delivery pipe from the right-hand side of the instrument.

4   Release the single cross-head screw which secures the carburettor top and withdraw the throttle valve assembly. This can be left connected to the cable unless it requires specific attention, in which case the return spring should be held against the carburettor top and the cable disengaged. The component parts can then be freed from the cable.

5   The carburettor body can now be freed from the intake adaptor. Slacken the clamp screw which secures the carburettor and pull the instrument clear of the adaptor.

6   The carburettor is refitted by reversing the removal sequence, paying particular attention to the fitting of the various hoses. The small oil delivery pipe should be primed with two-stroke oil to ensure immediate lubrication when the engine is started. This is best achieved using a pressure oil can. Check and adjust the throttle cable free play to give 1 - 2 mm movement at the adjuster. Once this has been set, remove the oil pump cover and check that the cross-headed pin and the alignment mark on the pulley coincide when the throttle cable play has **just** been taken up by turning the twistgrip. Any necessary adjustment of the oil pump cable can be made using the in-line adjuster provided below the front cowl.

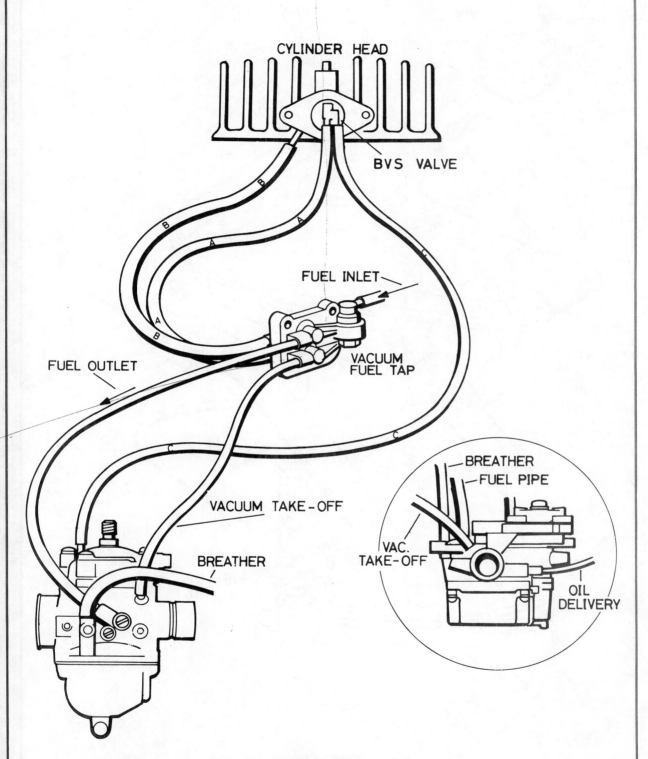

Fig. 2.1 BVS valve pipe connections

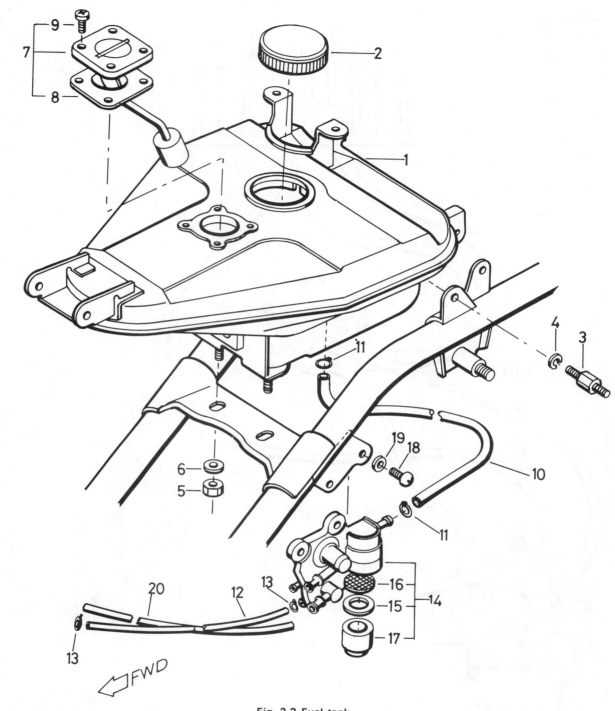

Fig. 2.2 Fuel tank

1 Fuel tank	8 Gasket	15 Sealing ring
2 Filler cap	9 Screw – 4 off	16 Gauze filter
3 Stud – 2 off	10 Fuel feed pipe	17 Filter cup
4 Spring washer – 2 off	11 Pipe clip – 2 off	18 Screw – 2 off
5 Nut – 2 off	12 Vacuum pipe	19 Spring washer – 2 off
6 Washer – 2 off	13 Pipe clip – 2 off	20 Fuel delivery pipe
7 Fuel gauge assembly	14 Vacuum fuel tap assembly	

FWD

6 Carburettor: dismantling, examination and reassembly

Note: For information on the automatic choke mechanism refer to Section 8.

1 Remove the four float bowl retaining screws and lift the bowl away, taking care not to damage the gasket. Displace the float pivot pin and remove the float together with the float needle. Unscrew the hexagon-headed main jet from the underside of the needle jet, followed by the needle jet itself. The pilot jet is located in the adjacent bore and can be removed with the aid of a screwdriver. If it is wished to remove the throttle stop screw or the pilot screw note the setting of each so that they can be refitted at the same setting. This can be done by screwing each one inwards until it seats lightly, counting the number of turns and part turns. The procedure is reversed during reassembly.

2 Carefully clean each part and check for wear or damage. The jets are best cleaned with a blast of compressed air from a low pressure air line or failing that, a foot pump. Where stubborn obstructions are encountered, a fine nylon bristle may be used as a last resort, but on no account should wire be used. The jets are soft and the precision drillings are easily scratched or enlarged, either of which will upset the carburation. Examine the jet needle for wear which will show up as scuff marks on one side of the needle. If visibly worn the needle must be renewed together with the needle jet which will be correspondingly worn. It is not practicable to measure wear in the needle jet, but if the needle is marked the jet will almost certainly have become oval.

3 Check the needle for straightness by rolling it on a sheet of plate glass. If any distortion is evident, the needle must be renewed. Examine the throttle valve for wear or score marks along its length. Provided that the air cleaner has been regularly maintained little wear will be found, but where this has occured, check the corresponding carburettor bore for wear at the same time. In very extreme cases it may be necessary to renew the throttle valve and the carburettor body to obviate air leakage between them, though it is usually sufficient to fit a new throttle valve.

4 The carburettor can be rebuilt by reversing the dismantling sequence, taking particular care to ensure that each component is spotlessly clean. When fitting the throttle stop and mixture screws, turn them inwards until they seat lightly, then back each one off to the position noted during dismantling. Check the condition of all O-rings and sealing washers, and renew any which have become marked or compressed. When fitting the jets take great care not to overtighten them. The soft brass material is easily fractured.

7 Automatic choke: dismantling, examination and reassembly

1 The automatic choke consists of a spring loaded plunger which opens an additional fuel circuit to provide the necessary fuel-rich mixture required for cold starting. The plunger remains in the 'On' position until the engine reaches normal operating temperature, when a heat sensing bi-metallic strip in the BVS valve opens to apply vacuum pressure to the auto-choke diaphragm. The reduced pressure below the diaphragm allows atmospheric pressure to overcome the spring pressure holding the plunger open, thus closing the cold start circuit.

2 The single most likely problem with this system is leakage, either in one of the vacuum pipes or because the diaphragm has split. The result of this would be that the plunger would fail to return to the 'Off' position and the engine would begin to run very roughly as it reached normal operating temperature, due to the excessively rich mixture. Eventually, the engine would stall and probably refuse to re-start until cold.

3 Check the pipe connections first, paying particular attention to the areas near the various mounting stubs. If cracks or splits are discovered, disconnect the pipe and cut off the last half inch or so, then refit it to restore the seal. If the pipes are in good condition the auto-choke diaphragm should be examined. Remove the two screws which retain the diaphragm cover. Take great care when removing the cover. The diaphragm will tend to stick to the sealing gasket and is easily damaged if removed carelessly. It is best to lift one corner and gradually peel the diaphragm off the cover.

4 The lower diaphragm is of more robust construction and is unlikely to give trouble. It is best checked in situ, since the plastic retaining ring is almost impossible to remove at home without causing damage to it or the carburettor body. It is recommended that if renewal of the lower diaphragm proves necessary, this operation is entrusted to a Yamaha Service Agent who will have the facilities to carry out the work without the risk of damage.

5 The automatic choke components can be fitted in the reverse of the dismantling order, taking care not to damage the delicate upper diaphragm. Make sure that there are no traces of dirt on the sealing faces.

6.2 Remove air cleaner trunking to expose carburettor

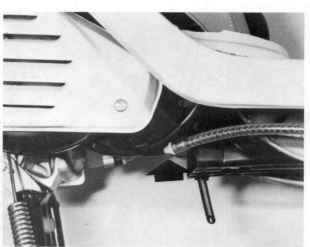

6.5 Oil delivery pipe **must** be primed after removal

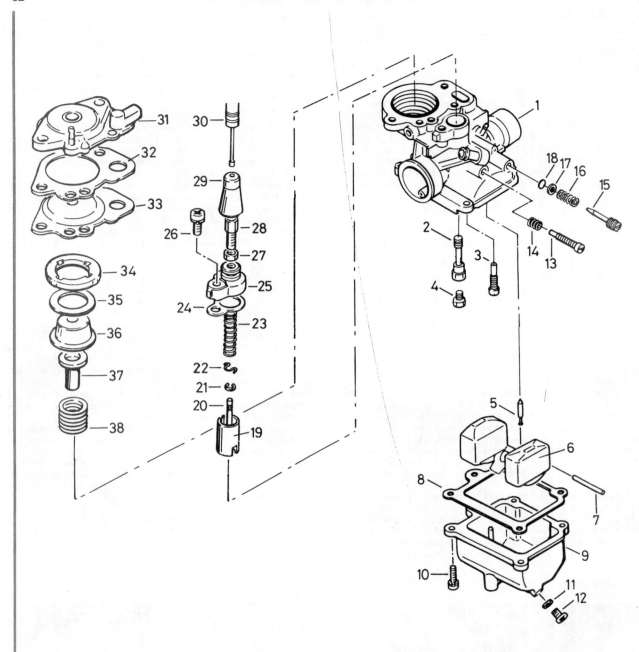

Fig. 2.3 Carburettor assembly

1 Carburettor body	14 Spring	27 Lock nut
2 Needle jet	15 Pilot screw	28 Cable adjuster
3 Pilot jet	16 Spring	29 Rubber cover
4 Main jet	17 Washer	30 Throttle cable
5 Float needle	18 O-ring	31 Diaphragm cover
6 Float	19 Throttle valve	32 Gasket
7 Float pivot pin	20 Jet needle	33 Diaphragm
8 Gasket	21 Circlip	34 Plastic retaining ring
9 Float bowl	22 W-clip	35 Washer
10 Screw – 4 off	23 Spring	36 Lower diaphragm
11 Sealing washer	24 Gasket	37 Plunger
12 Drain screw	25 Carburettor top	38 Spring
13 Throttle stop screw	26 Screw	

7.1a Displace the float pivot pin ...

7.1b ... and remove the float and float needle

7.1c Main jet is screwed into underside of needle jet

7.1d Needle jet is removed as shown

7.1e Pilot jet has slotted head

7.1f The throttle stop screw (arrowed)

7.1g The pilot screw should be removed, after noting setting

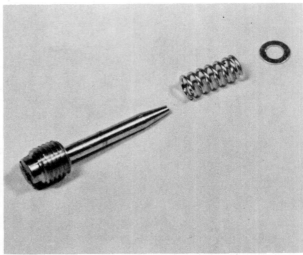

7.1h Note position of pilot screw, spring and washer

7.2a Check the condition of the jets ...

7.2b ... clearing them with compressed air

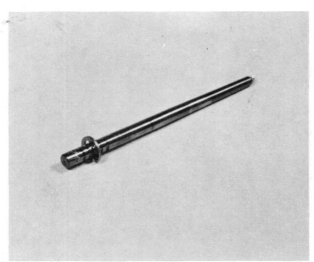

7.2c Needle must be renewed if bent or scored

7.3 Examine throttle valve for wear marks

7.4a Float needle should be renewed if tip is worn

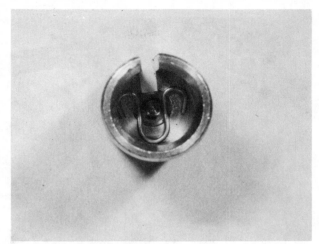

7.4b Note position of needle retaining clip

7.4c Check the condition of float bowl gasket

8 Carburettor: settings and adjustment

1   The carburettor fitted to the Passola model is of the conventional slide type in which the basic mixture settings are controlled by a combination of jet sizes and needle position. These are given in the specifications section at the beginning of this Chapter and should not normally require any modification. If the carburettor is stripped in an attempt to rectify running faults it is important that all jets and settings are restored to those specified, and any worn components renewed. It is almost impossible to tune a carburettor which is worn or incorrectly jetted, and at best any such attempt can only compensate for basic faults.

2   When checking jet sizes it should be noted that the pilot jet size must match the various float bowls which may be fitted. This can be deduced by checking the float bowl part number and comparing it with the table below:

Float bowl part number	Pilot jet size
2T4 - 14381 - 20	40
2T4 - 14381 - 21	42
2T4 - 14381 - 22	44

A similar range of main jets is listed by the manufacturer, the standard item being 94, with optional sizes of 92 and 96. Unfortunately, no information is available which would indicate whether the main jet size relates to the float bowl number in the same manner as has been described above for the pilot jet. Note

that the main jet size for non-UK machines fitted with the Teikei Y8P carburettor is 74.

3   If persistent flooding occurs which cannot be traced to a worn float needle, or if continual over-richness or weakness is experienced the float height should be checked. To make the check the carburettor must be detached and the float chamber removed. Measure the distance between the top surface of the floats and the mating surface of the carburettor as shown in the accompanying illustration. The carburettor should be inverted during the check so that the float needle is seated lightly but the needle spring is not compressed. If the float height is not within the specified range of 25 ± 1 mm (0.9843 ± 0.0394 in) adjustment may be made by bending the float tang a small amount.

4   The pilot mixture and idle speed can be adjusted as follows. Run the engine until it reaches normal operating temperature, noting that this is best done by riding the machine for a few miles. Identify the pilot air screw and the throttle stop screw, both of which are fitted to the left-hand side of the instrument. The pilot air screw is the higher of the two and is fitted into a tubular extension of the carburettor body. The throttle stop screw is mounted lower and has a large slotted cheese head.

5   **Important note:** before undertaking any adjustment work with the engine running it is essential that it is remembered that the Passola has an automatic transmisison system. It will be appreciated that as the idle speed rises the centrifugal clutch will engage and the machine will attempt to move off. Be particularly wary of inadvertently 'blipping' the throttle. The machine should be placed squarely on its centre stand, checkng that the rear wheel is raised clear of the ground, before work commences.

6   Start the engine and allow it to idle. Starting from the nominal setting of $1\frac{1}{2}$ - $1\frac{3}{4}$ turns out, move the pilot air screw by about $\frac{1}{2}$ turn and note its effect on the idle speed. Turn it a further $\frac{1}{2}$ turn and again note its effect on the idle speed. By this method it is possible to establish the exact setting at which the engine tickover is fastest and most regular, this position normally coinciding with the recommended nominal setting. There is normally a band of adjustment covering one or two turns each side of the optimum setting. Once the pilot mixture strength has been set, adjust the throttle stop screw to give a reasonably slow but reliable tickover.

7   Further modifications to the carburettor settings such as changes of jet size or needle position are not likely to be necessary under normal circumstances. If carburation problems should arise do not forget that a dirty air cleaner element or choked exhaust system can often be traced as the source of the trouble, and these areas should be checked first. See Sections 12 and 13 for details.

8.3a Diaphragm cover is retained by two screws

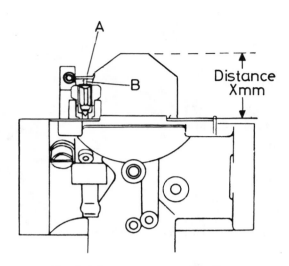

Fig. 2.4 Checking the float height

A   *Float tongue*
B   *Float valve*
X = 25 ± 1 mm (0.9843 ± 0.0394 in)

8.3b Remove cover and check gaskets and diaphragm

9 Reed valve induction system: mode of operation

1   Of the various systems of controlling the induction cycle of a two-stroke engine, Yamaha has chosen to adopt the reed valve, a device which permits precise control of the incoming mixture, allowing more favourable port timing to give improved torque and power outputs. The reed valve assembly comprises a wedge-shaped die-cast aluminium alloy valve case mounted in the inlet tract. The valve case has rectangular ports which are closed off by flexible stainless steel reeds. The reeds seal against a heat and oil resistent synthetic rubber gasket which is bonded to the valve case. A specially shaped valve stopper, made from cold rolled stainless steel plate, controls the extent of movement of the valve reeds.
2   As the piston ascends in the cylinder, a partial vacuum is formed beneath the cylinder in the crankcase. This allows atmospheric pressure to force the valves open, and a fresh charge of petrol/air mixture flows past the valve and into the crankcase. As the pressure differential becomes equalised, the valves close, and the incoming charge is then trapped. The charge of mixture in the cylinder is by this time fully compressed, and ignition takes place driving the piston downwards. The descending piston eventually uncovers the exhaust port, and the hot exhaust gases, still under a certain amount of pressure, are discharged into the exhaust system. At this stage, the reed valve, in conjunction with the 7th, or auxiliary scavenging port, performs a secondary function; as the hot exhaust gases rush out of the exhaust port, a momentary depression is created in the cylinder, this allows the valve to open once more, but this time the incoming mixture enters directly into the cylinder via the 7th port and completes the expulsion of the now inert burnt gases. This ensures that the cylinder is filled with the maximum possible combustion mixture. The charge of combustion mixture which has been compressed in the crankcase is released into the cylinder via the transfer ports, and the piston again ascends to close the various ports and begin compression. The reed valves open once more as another partial vacuum is created in the crankcase, and the cycle of induction thus repeats. It will be noted that no direct mechanical operation of the valve takes place, the pressure differential being the sole controlling factor.

8.3c Do not attempt to remove lower diaphragm at home

10 Reed valve: removal, examination and renovation

1   The reed valve assembly is a precision component, and as such should not be dismantled unnecessarily. The valves are located in the inlet tract, covered by the carburettor flange.
2   Remove the carburettor as described in Chapter 2, Section 6, thus exposing the four cross-headed screws retaining the reed valve assemblies to the crankcase. After removing the screws, the assembly can be carefully lifted away.
3   The valve can now be washed in clean petrol to facilitate further examination. It should be handled with great care, and on no account dropped. The stainless steel reeds should be inspected for signs of cracking or fatigue, and if suspect should be renewed. Remember that any part of the assembly which breaks off in service will almost certainly be drawn into the engine, causing extensive damage.
4   Note the position of the reed in relation to the Neoprene bonded gasket against which it seats. It should be flush to form an effective seal. If further dismantling is deemed necessary proceed as follows.
5   Remove the two cross-headed screws securing the valve stopper and reed to the case. Handle the reed carefully, avoiding bending, and note from which side it was removed. All components should be replaced in their original positions. Lay the reed carefully to one side if it is to be re-used. Examine the Neoprene seating face which, if defective, will necessitate the replacement of the complete alloy case, to which it is heat-bonded.
6   Reassembly is a direct reversal of the dismantling process. Clean all parts thoroughly, but gently, before refitting. A thread locking compound, such as Loctite, must be applied to the two cross-headed screws, which should be tightened progressively to avoid warping the reed or stopper. Do not omit the locking compound, as the screws retain a component which vibrates many times each second and consequently are prone to loosening if assembled incorrectly.

11 Air filter: removal, cleaning and reassembly

1   The air filter consists of a moulded plastic casing containing an oil-impregnated foam element. Access to the air filter is gained after the front cowl section immediately below the seat has been removed. This is retained by the two lower side panel screws plus a single control screw. Once the cowl has been removed, pull off the moulded hose which connects the air filter to the carburettor to expose the single screw which secures the air filter cover.
2   Carefully remove the flat foam element from the casing, taking care not to tear the foam. The element can be cleaned by washing it thoroughly in petrol to remove all traces of old oil and accumulated dust. Squeeze out any residual petrol and allow the element to dry before re-impregnating it with clean two-stroke oil. The element should then be wrapped in some clean rag and squeezed to remove any excess oil.
3   Fit the cleaned and re-oiled element in the reverse of the dismantling order, ensuring that the element fits correctly and that there is no chance of air leakage around it. It should be noted that small two-stroke engines of this type are very sensitive to air filter condition. As the filter becomes choked, the efficiency of the engine will be reduced and fuel consumption will increase. Eventually the engine will begin to run badly, but this will only become evident after the element has become severely choked. It follows that regular cleaning is essential and that the filter condition should be checked whenever poor performance is evident.

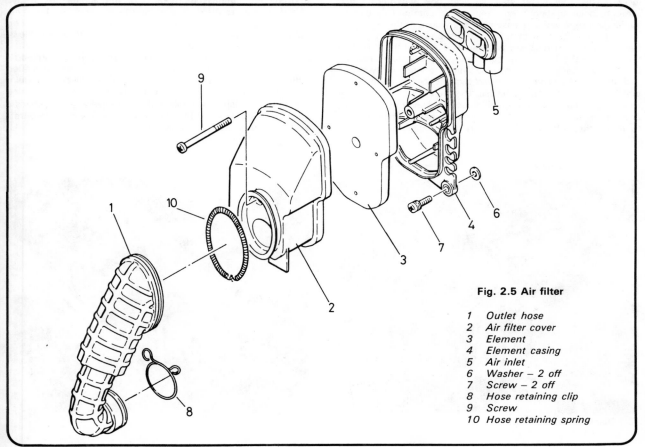

Fig. 2.5 Air filter

1   Outlet hose
2   Air filter cover
3   Element
4   Element casing
5   Air inlet
6   Washer – 2 off
7   Screw – 2 off
8   Hose retaining clip
9   Screw
10 Hose retaining spring

11.3 The reed valve assembly

12 Exhaust system: removal and maintenance

1   The exhaust system of the Passola is of one piece construction, the exhaust pipe being welded directly to the pressed steel silencer box. When new, the system is protected by a high temperature paint finish which prevents rusting, but in time this will begin to flake off leaving the silencer unprotected. If ignored, the thin sheet steel silencer box will quickly rust through, necessitating a new replacement item. This can be avoided by removing the assembly every six months or so. The silencer and pipe can then be cleaned and degreased and a fresh coat of heat resistant paint applied. One of the very high temperature (VHT) coatings such as Sperex is recommended.
2   The silencer and exhaust pipe unit is retained by two nuts and studs at the exhaust port and two silencer mounting bolts which secure it to the crankcase. It should be noted that the exhaust port flange nuts are well recessed below the crankcase, and will require a socket and an extension bar or a box spanner to reach them. It is not necessary to remove the nuts and

washers to free the exhaust pipe from the exhaust port, the flange being slotted to permit removal once the nuts have been slackened. If the two silencer bolts are now removed the unit can be disengaged from the engine and removed.
3   Degrease and clean the silencer body and exhaust pipe, using a wire brush to remove any loose rust. Once clean, coat the unit in heat resistant paint, following the manufacturer's directions. Before the system is refitted check for and remove any build-up of carbon in the silencer tailpipe. When fitting the silencer make sure that a *new* exhaust port sealing ring is used to avoid any leakage. It was found to be helpful to retain the ring on the exhaust pipe flange with one or two spots of iso-cyanoacrylate adhesive (Superglue or similar).

13 Oil pump: general description and adjustment

1   Unlike many two-strokes, the Yamaha Passola has an independent lubrication system for the engine and does not require the mixture of a measured quantity of oil to the petrol content of the fuel tank in order to utilise the so-called 'petroil' method. Oil of the correct viscosity (Yamaha Autolube oil, or an equivalent two-stroke oil) is contained in a separate oil tank mounted at the rear of the machine and is fed to a mechanical oil pump on the front of the engine which is driven from the crankshaft by reduction gear. The pump delivers oil at a predetermined rate, via a rubber tube, to oilways in the inlet side of the carburettor. In consequence, the oil is carried into the engine by the incoming charge of petrol vapour, when the inlet port opens.
2   The oil pump is also interconnected to the twist grip throttle, so that when the throttle is opened, the oil pump setting is increased a similar amount. This technique ensures that the lubrication requirements of the engine are always directly related to the degree of throttle opening. This facility is arranged by means of a control cable looped around a pulley on the end of the pump; the cable is joined to the throttle cable at a junction box beneath the floor board.
3   The system is reliable and accurate, removing the problems of fouled spark plugs and smoking exhausts often associated with two-stroke engines. The pump itself is unlikely to require attention during the life of the machine, other than routine adjustment which synchronises the oil delivery rate to specific engine speeds. This must be carried out whenever the carburettor or oil pump have been disturbed.

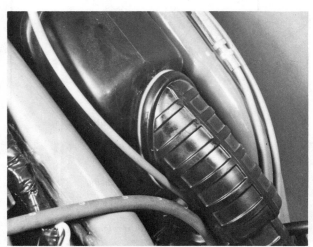

12.1 Displace air cleaner trunking ...

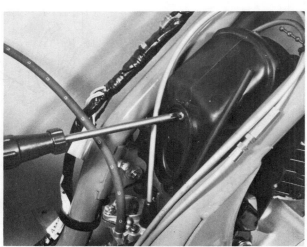

12.2 ... to reach cover securing screw

4   Remove the small plastic oil pump cover so that the pump pulley is visible. Start the engine and allow it to warm up to normal operating temperature. This is important to ensure that the auto-choke is off and the engine is running at its normal idle speed. Gradually open the throttle twistgrip until the engine speed **just** begins to increase, indicating that the free play in the throttle cable has been taken up. At this setting the pin and fixed pointer on the oil pump should coincide. If necessary, make any adjustments using the in-line adjuster fitted to the clutch cable next to the air filter unit. **Note**: Take great care not to open the throttle twistgrip too far, otherwise the automatic transmission will engage. For this reason, place the machine securely on its centre stand and make sure that tools or other items are kept clear of the rear wheel.

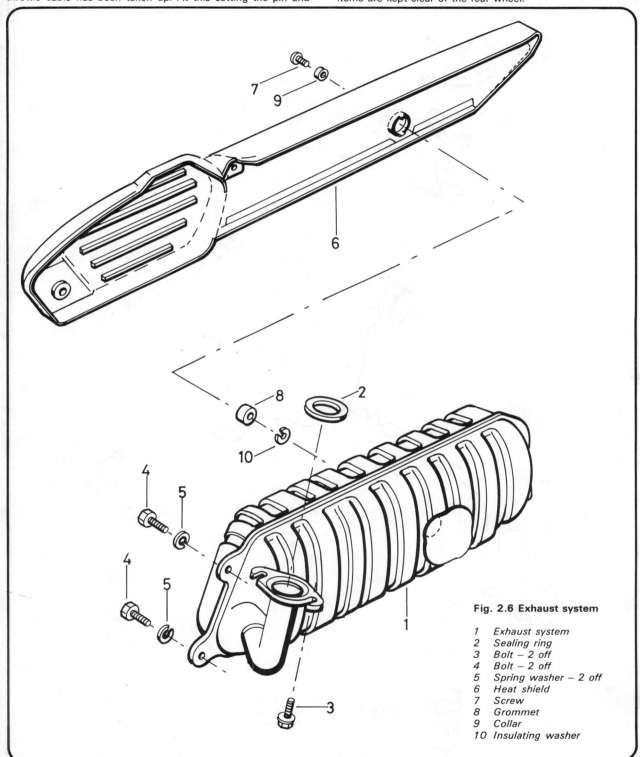

Fig. 2.6 Exhaust system

1   Exhaust system
2   Sealing ring
3   Bolt – 2 off
4   Bolt – 2 off
5   Spring washer – 2 off
6   Heat shield
7   Screw
8   Grommet
9   Collar
10   Insulating washer

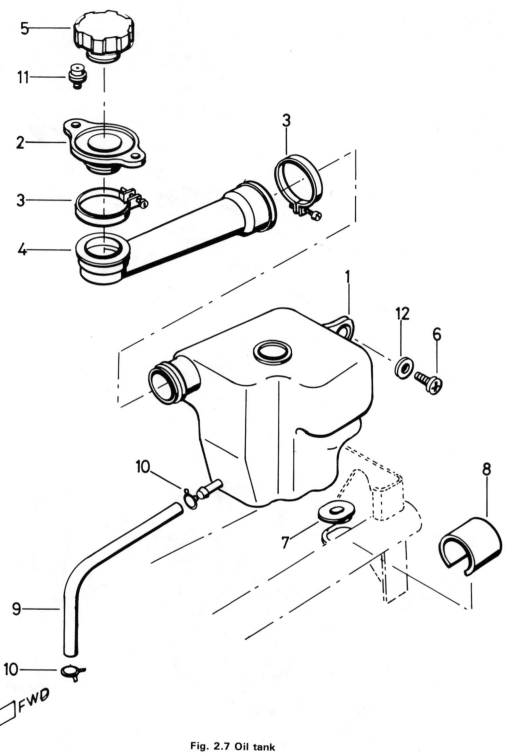

Fig. 2.7 Oil tank

1	Oil tank	7	Grommet
2	Flange	8	Rubber cushion
3	Hose clamp – 2 off	9	Oil feed pipe
4	Connecting hose	10	Pipe clip
5	Filler cap	11	Screw and washer – 2 off
6	Screw	12	Collar

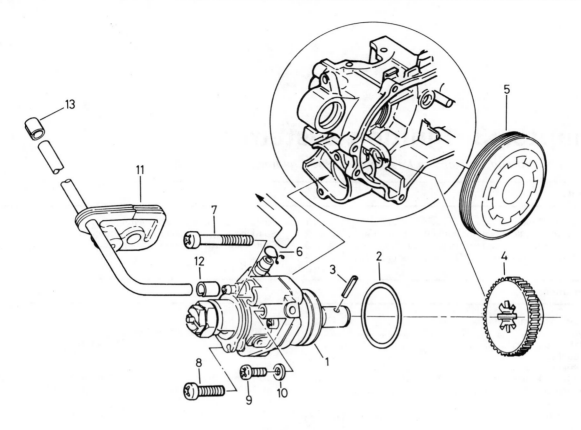

Fig. 2.8 Oil pump

1 Oil pump	6 Hose clip	10 Sealing washer
2 O-ring	7 Screw	11 Grommet
3 Roll pin	8 Screw	12 Spring collar
4 Driven pinion	9 Bleed screw	13 Spring collar
5 Drive pinion		

14 Fault diagnosis: fuel system

Symptom	Cause	Remedy
Excessive fuel consumption	Air cleaner choked or restricted	Clean or renew element
	Fuel leaking from carburettor	Check all unions and gaskets
	Badly worn or distorted carburettor	Renew
Idling speed too high	Throttle stop screw in too far	Adjust screw
	Carburettor top loose	Tighten
	Auto-choke system faulty	Check and overhaul
Engine sluggish. Does not respond to throttle	Back pressure in silencer	Check and clean if necessary
	Air cleaner choked or restricted	Check and clean if necessary
	Auto-choke system faulty	Check and overhaul
Engine dies after running for a short while	Dirt or water in carburettor	Remove and clean
General lack of performance	Weak mixture: float needle sticking in seat	Remove float chamber and check needle seating
	Air leak at carburettor or leaking crankcase seals	Check for air leaks or worn seals

Chapter 3 Ignition system

For information and revisions to later models, see Chapter 7

Contents

Specifications

Ignition system

Type	CDI (capacitor discharge ignition)	
Make	Yamaha	Mitsubishi
Model	F2T4	–
Voltage	6	6
Pulser coil resistance	20 ohm ± 10%	90 ohm ± 10%
Source coil resistance	300 ohm ± 10%	290 ohm ± 10%

Ignition timing .... 21° BTDC @ 5000 rpm – non-adjustable

Ignition coil

Make	Yamaha	Mitsubishi
Type	C2T4	–
* Primary winding resistance	1.6 ohm ± 10%	1.0 ohm ± 10%
* Secondary winding resistance	6..6 Kohm ± 20%	5.9 ohm ± 20%

*Note: *Measurement at 20°C (68°F)*

CDI unit

Make	Yamaha
Type	2E9

Sparking plug

Make	NGK	Nippondenso	Champion
Type	BP4HS	W14FP-UL	L86C
Gap	0.6 – 0.7 mm (0.024 – 0.028 in)		

1 General description

The Passola features what amounts to a maintenance-free electronic ignition system in which there are no moving parts and thus no mechanical wear. The CDI (capacitor discharge ignition) system comprises a solid state CDI unit and a magnetic pickup assembly. The latter replaces the traditional contact breaker assembly as the means of switching the ignition spark.

As the generator rotor rotates current is generated in the ignition source coil which is transferred to and stored in the capacitor in the CDI unit. As the generator rotor moves further a trigger current is produced in the magnetic pick-up assembly which signals the stored power in the capacitor to discharge through the primary windings of the ignition coil. This surge of current induces a high voltage discharge from the ignition coil which is fed via the HT lead to produce the spark across the sparking plug electrodes.

2 Checking the ignition system: general information

1 The CDI system is designed to required no regular maintenance, with the exception of the sparking plug which should be cleaned and adjusted at the intervals specified in Routine Maintenance. In the event that the system fails it is likely that the fault lies in one of the associated wiring connections rather than the CDI unit or pickup assembly, and the various terminals, connector blocks and the ignition switch should be checked first.

2 It should be noted that access to the pickup assembly and generator stator components will require the removal of the flywheel rotor. It was found that it is necessary to use the correct manufacturer's extractor, part number 90890-01189, for this operation, there being no safe alternative method of rotor removal. Care must be taken when checking the system to avoid electric shocks. The CDI unit produces high voltages which can prove dangerous. It should be noted that the CDI

unit, the pulser coil assembly and the ignition coil are all sealed units and in the event of a fault repair is impracticable. Where a fault is suspected it is recommended that the unit is taken to a Yamaha Service Agent for final checking before a replacement unit is purchased.

3   A limited range of tests are possible using a multimeter. These are described in the text for the benefit of owners suitably equipped and conversant with the use of these instruments. If in any doubt it is recommended that the assistance of a Yamaha Service Agent is sought.

3   Checking the ignition system: tracing wiring faults

1   As mentioned, the single most likely cause of ignition failure is a damaged or broken wiring connection. It is assumed that the sparking plug has been removed and checked by substitution to eliminate it as the source of the problem. Where possible, a multimeter set on the resistance position should be used to establish the likely location of the faulty connection. Failing this, connect up a dry battery and bulb as shown in Fig. 3.2. The two probe leads can be fitted with small crocodile clips and can be connected to either end of a circuit to indicate continuity by lighting the bulb. This latter method will work just as well as a multimeter in this application, but whichever method is chosen it is recommended that the machine's electrical system is isolated by disconnecting the battery.

2   The wiring can be checked in conjunction with the wiring diagram at the back of the manual. Start by testing the black/red lead at the bullet connector next to the air cleaner. The connector should be separated and one of the probe leads connected to its male end, this being the lead which runs to the ignition switch. If the remaining probe is connected to earth, a completed circuit should be indicated when the ignition switch is 'Off'. Try turning the switch to the 'On' position which should result in the circuit being broken. If this is not the case it will indicate that the circuit has shorted at some point. This will mean that the ignition system is permanently earthed and thus inoperative, and may be due to a damaged area of the wiring insulation, or water or internal shorting of the switch itself. The switch unit is sealed and cannot be dismantled for cleaning. If it proves to be faulty try cleaning it with a contact cleaner or an aerosol product such as WD 40. If these fail to effect a cure, a new switch will be required.

3   Test the remaining wiring runs by connecting a probe lead to each end to check continuity, and by connecting one probe to the lead and the other to earth to check for short circuits. Visually examine all connections and terminals for signs of corrosion or arcing, cleaning or renewing these as required. If no faults are discovered in the wiring, connections or switch, it can be assumed that the fault must lie in the CDI unit, pickup assembly or coil.

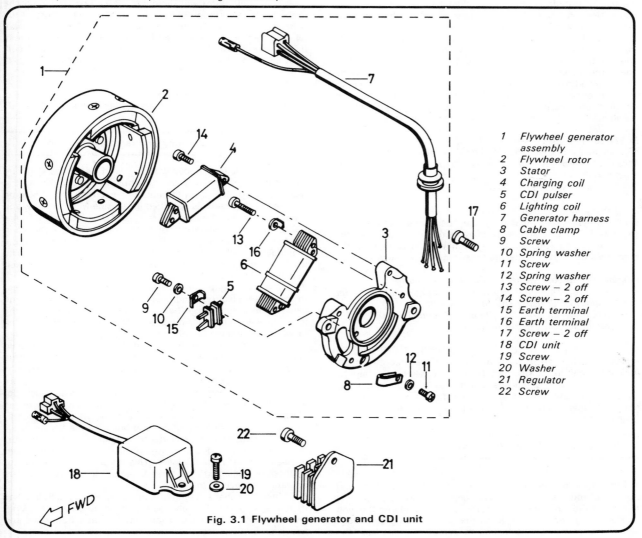

1   Flywheel generator assembly
2   Flywheel rotor
3   Stator
4   Charging coil
5   CDI pulser
6   Lighting coil
7   Generator harness
8   Cable clamp
9   Screw
10 Spring washer
11 Screw
12 Spring washer
13 Screw – 2 off
14 Screw – 2 off
15 Earth terminal
16 Earth terminal
17 Screw – 2 off
18 CDI unit
19 Screw
20 Washer
21 Regulator
22 Screw

FWD

Fig. 3.1 Flywheel generator and CDI unit

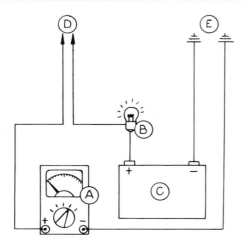

Fig. 3.2 Method of checking the machine's wiring

A   Multimeter
B   Bulb
C   Battery
D   Positive probe
E   Negative probe

4   Ignition system: testing the CDI components

1   A limited amount of testing can be undertaken to check the serviceability of the pulser coil and the CDI source coil, given the use of a multimeter capable of making measurements in ohms. Note that the kilo ohms (ohms x 1000) scale found on many of the smaller meters cannot be used for this purpose.

2   Trace the output leads from the flywheel generator back to the connector beneath the front cowl. Separate the connector and identify that white/red lead from the pulser coil. Connect one of the meter probes to this terminal and the other to earth. The specified resistance should be as shown in the table below. In the event of failure it is likely that the coil will have short circuited (no resistance) or have gone open circuit (infinite resistance). In either case renewal will be necessary.

Pulser coil resistance (White/red lead to earth)
Figures are for the Yamaha F2T4 flywheel generator. Where the Mitsubishi flywheel generator is fitted refer to figures in brackets
    20 ohms (9 ohms) ± 10%

3   The ignition source coil resistance can be checked in a similar manner by measuring the resistance between the separate Black/red lead and earth. Note that the ignition switch must be turned 'On' for this test, having disconnected the machine's battery. The specified resistance is as shown below.

Ignition source coil resistance (Black/red to earth)
Figures are for the Yamaha F2T4 flywheel generator, those for the Mitsubishi unit being shown in brackets
    Ignition switch 'On' 300 ohms (290 ohms) ± 10%
    Ignition switch 'Off' No resistance

4   The machine is fitted with a Yamaha 2E9 CDI unit, for which no test information is available. If the preceding tests indicate a fault in the CDI unit it should be taken to a Yamaha Service Agent who should be able to verify its condition and supply a new unit if necessary. Repair of the sealed CDI unit is not practicable. For details of ignition coil tests refer to Section 5 of this Chapter.

5   Ignition coil: location and testing

1   The ignition or high tension (HT) coil is located immediately in front of the oil tank and can be reached after the right-hand side panel and the rear cowl have been removed. Its purpose is to convert the pulse transmitted from the CDI unit into the high tension pulse necessary to jump the sparking plug electrodes and cause ignition of the fuel/air mixture. The pulse from the

CDI unit creates a brief magnetic field in the primary windings of the ignition coil which induces a high tension pulse in the secondary windings which is fed in turn to the sparking plug.

2   To test the ignition coil it is necessary to measure the resistance of the primary and secondary windings using a multimeter with ohms and kilo ohms scales. Connect one of the probe leads to earth, preferably the laminated steel core of the coil, and the other to the thin orange lead for the primary winding test or to the HT lead for the secondary winding test. In the table below the readings are for the Yamaha C2T4 coil, with the Mitsubishi unit figures shown in brackets.

Ignition coil resistance tests
    Primary windings 1.6 ohms (1.0 ohms) ± 10%
    Secondary windings 6.6 k ohms (5.9 k ohms) ± 10%

6   Sparking plug: checking and resetting the gap

1   The Passola is equipped with an NGK BP4HS sparking plug as standard equipment, the Champion L-89CM being the recommended alternative fitment. The electrode gap should be checked at the intervals specified in Routine Maintenance, and must be maintained within the range of 0.6 – 0.7 mm (0.024 – 0.028 in). Certain operating conditions may indicate a change in sparking plug grade, although the type recommended by the manufacturer will usually give the best, all round service. The use of anything other than the recommended grade may result in a holed piston.

2   To reset the gap, bend the outer electrode to bring it closer to the centre electrode and check that the correct feeler gauge can be inserted. Never bend the central electrode or the insulator will crack, causing engine damage if the particles fall in whilst the engine is running.

3   With some experience, the condition of the sparking plug electrode and insulator can be used as a reliable guide to engine operating conditions. See accompanying colour photographs.

4   Beware of overtightening the sparking plug otherwise there is risk of stripping the threads from the aluminium alloy cylinder head. The plug should be sufficiently tight to sit firmly on its sealing washer, and no more. Use a spanner which is a good fit to prevent the spanner slipping and breaking the insulator.

5   If the threads in the cylinder head strip as a result of over-tightening the sparking plug, it is possible to reclaim the head by use of a Helicoil thread insert. This is a cheap and convenient method of replacing the threads; most motorcycle dealers operate a service of this kind.

6   Make sure that the plug insulating cap is a good fit and has its rubber seal. It should also be kept clean to prevent tracking. The cap contains the suppressor that eliminates both radio and television interference.

Spark plug maintenance: Checking plug gap with feeler gauges

Altering the plug gap. Note use of correct tool

Spark plug conditions: A brown, tan or grey firing end is indicative of correct engine running conditions and the selection of the appropriate heat rating plug

White deposits have accumulated from excessive amounts of oil in the combustion chamber or through the use of low quality oil. Remove deposits or a hot spot may form

Black sooty deposits indicate an over-rich fuel/air mixture, or a malfunctioning ignition system. If no improvement is obtained, try one grade hotter plug

Wet, oily carbon deposits form an electrical leakage path along the insulator nose, resulting in a misfire. The cause may be a badly worn engine or a malfunctioning ignition system

A blistered white insulator or melted electrode indicates over-advanced ignition timing or a malfunctioning cooling system. If correction does not prove effective, try a colder grade plug

A worn spark plug not only wastes fuel but also overloads the whole ignition system because the increased gap requires higher voltage to initiate the spark. This condition can also affect air pollution

4.4 CDI unit location (arrowed)

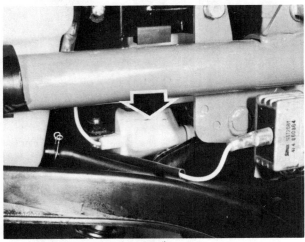

5.1 Ignition coil location (arrowed)

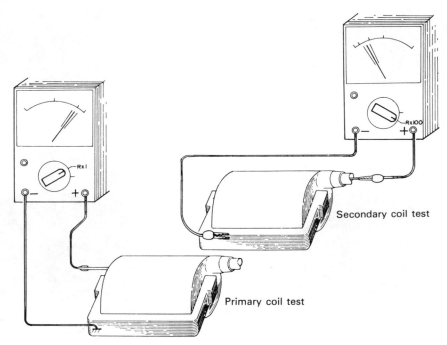

Secondary coil test

Primary coil test

Fig. 3.3 Ignition coil test

---

7 Fault diagnosis: ignition system

Symptom	Cause	Remedy
Engine will not start — no spark at plug	Red/black lead from ignition switch earthed	Check switch and connectors for water contamination or damage Check that lead has not worn through on frame
	Plug faulty or oiled up	Remove and check by substitution. Clean and re-gap plug
— weak spark at plug	See above	See above
	CDI system or HT coil faulty	Refer to main text
Engine starts, but runs poorly	Intermittent or weak spark	Check sparking plug condition as described above. Check ignition system connections Check ignition coil
	Carburation fault	Refer to Chapter 2

Chapter 4 Frame and forks

For information and revisions to later models, see Chapter 7

Contents

Specifications

Frame
Type .... Welded tubular steel

Forks
Type .... Undamped telescopic
Travel .... 45 mm (1.7717 in)

Rear suspension
Type .... Pivoted engine/transmission unit, single suspension unit
Suspension unit .... Coil spring and damper, non-adjustable
Suspension unit travel .... 45 mm (1.7717 in)
Rear wheel travel .... 58 mm (2.2835 in)

Torque settings

	kgf m	lbf ft
Handlebar retaining bolt	2.8	20.3
Steering stem locknut	3.5	25.3
Fuel tank mounting bolts	1.8	13.0
Rear suspension mounting (upper)	2.3	16.6
Rear suspension mounting (lower)	1.8	13.0

1 General description

The Passola features an open scooter-type frame consisting of two tubes running from the rear lamp area forward to the floorboard. At this point the two tubes converge and are attached to a single large diameter tube which runs up to, and supports, the steering head. The assembly is strengthened by numerous gussets and braces.

The front forks comprise a tubular steering column which terminates in a fabricated bottom bracket. This in turn supports the two tubular fork tubes. The lower legs run inside these tubes and are supported by coil springs to provide front suspension. The right-hand fork incorporates a rubber cone type bump stop. The forks are undamped.

Rear suspension is by swinging arm, the arm in this instance being formed by the engine/transmission unit. Two large lugs on the front of the crankcase carry a sealed journal ball bearing between which runs a hollow pivot tube. A large bolt secures the assembly to the front engine mounting. The latter incorporates a rather ingenious arrangement to absorb engine vibration which would otherwise be transmitted to the frame. This is accomplished by incorporating a pivot arrangement in the mounting assembly, vibrations being absorbed by small compression springs.

2 Frame and fork overhaul: general information

1   It should be noted that most of the machine is covered by removable panels, necessitating a certain amount of preliminary dismantling before the component in question can be reached. It is worth remembering that many of these panels are of soft plastic construction, and may be damaged if not removed and placed to one side. Full details of bodywork removal are given in Chapter 1 Section 3.

3 Front fork assembly: removal and refitting

1   The front forks are removed as an assembly together with the steering stem. To gain access to the steering stem area it will first be necessary to remove the legshield and steering

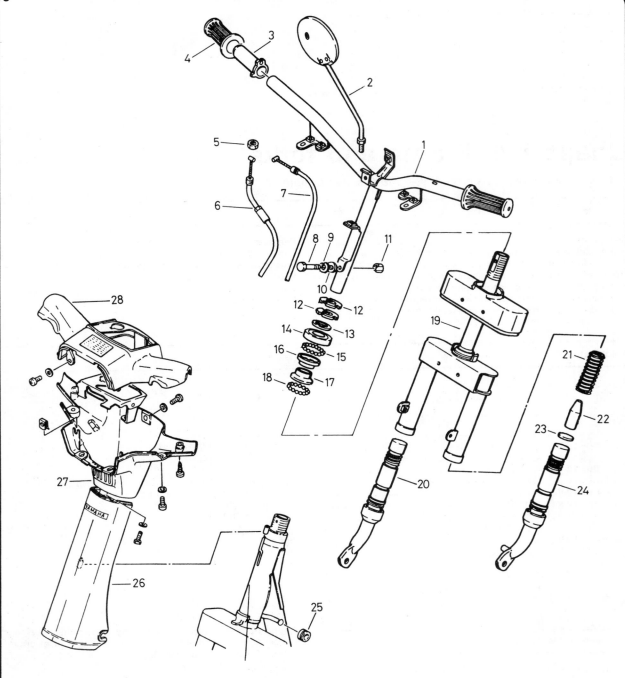

Fig. 4.1 Front forks and steering assembly

1	Handlebar	11	Nut	20	Right-hand fork leg
2	Rear view mirror	12	Slotted nut – 2 off	21	Fork spring
3	Throttle twistgrip inner	13	Washer	22	Rubber bump stop
4	Throttle twistgrip	14	Upper bearing cone	23	Spring seat
5	Nut	15	Steel balls	24	Left-hand fork leg
6	Throttle cable	16	Upper bearing cup	25	Grommet
7	Front brake cable	17	Lower bearing cone	26	Steering column cover
8	Bolt	18	Steel balls	27	Handlebar lower cowling
9	Spring washer	19	Steering stem	28	Handlebar upper cowling
10	Washer				

column cover. The legshield is retained by screws which secure its lower edge to the floorboard, and by a single central screw which secures it to the steering head gusset plate. The steering column cover is clipped onto three mounting rubbers and can be pulled off.

2   Check that the machine is placed securely on its centre stand, then place wooden blocks or a jack beneath the floorboard brackets to raise the front wheel clear of the ground. Free the speedometer drive cable by displacing its retaining clip and pulling the end clear. Slacken and remove the front brake adjuster nut and disengage the cable and spring from the brake backplate. Straighten and withdraw the split pin which locks the front wheel spindle nut. The nut can now be removed and the spindle pulled clear to free the front wheel.

3   Remove the four cross-head screws which retain the basket and carrier assembly to the front forks, noting that it is not necessary to detach the basket from the carrier to effect removal. The front mudguard can now be removed by releasing its two mounting bolts which pass up into the fork. The handlebar assembly can be released as a unit from the steering stem after the single mounting bolt has been withdrawn. Remove the bolt and twist the assembly upwards until it comes free of the steering stem. Take care not to strain the control cables or electrical leads during this operation. The handlebar assembly can be rested on the frame until the forks are refitted.

4   Before any attempt is made to remove the fork assembly it should be noted that the steering head bearings are of the cup and cone type, each race containing 26 steel balls which will be freed as the steering column is removed from the headstock. The balls in the lower race in particular will tend to drop away as the steering stem is lowered, and some provision must be made to catch them. As a precautionary measure, place an old dust sheet or similar large piece of cloth beneath the steering head so that the balls do not strike a hard surface when they fall.

5   The steering stem is secured by two slotted nuts, the lower one being set to give the correct adjustment, whilst the upper one locks it in position. Using a C-spanner (*not* a hammer and punch) slacken and remove the locknut. The adjustment nut can now be removed, taking care to support the fork assembly so that the bearings are not exposed. Remove the upper cone, noting any of the bearing balls which might tend to stick to it. Carefully lower the fork assembly, trying as far as possible not to dislodge any of the lower bearing balls. Some of these will usually fall away onto the cloth, but the majority will tend to stay in place. The retaining balls from both races should be collected and placed in a tin or jar ready for cleaning.

6   The fork is assembled in the reverse of the dismantling order, having first degreased and cleaned the bearing races and

the balls. These must be in good condition, and if there is any sign of wear, corrosion or indentation the affected parts must be renewed. Apply a thick film of general purpose grease to the upper and lower cups and use this to hold the bearing balls in position, noting that 26 are fitted to each. There will be a small gap left when the balls are in place, this being allowed to prevent them skidding against each other in service. Do not attempt to fit any extra balls.

7   Feed the fork assembly into position, taking great care not to dislodge any of the balls. Lower the upper cone into position, then fit the adjustment nut to retain the assembly. Accurate setting of the latter is of great importance, since it is very easy to overtighten the assembly and thus place an unduly heavy load on the bearings. The nut should be turned until all discernible play has been taken up, but no more. Overtight head races will cause heavy steering, which could be dangerous, and will lead to rapid wear of the bearings. Hold the adjustment nut in this position and fit the locking nut which should be tightened securely onto it to lock the setting. Make a final check of adjustment to ensure that it is correct, then complete assembly of the ancillary parts in the reverse order of removal.

3.1 Steering head cover is clipped in place

3.3a Remove screws (arrowed) and lift basket and rack away

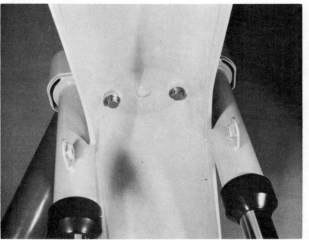

3.3b Front mudguard is retained by two bolts

3.3c Remove handlebar retaining bolt ...

3.3d ... and special threaded retainer

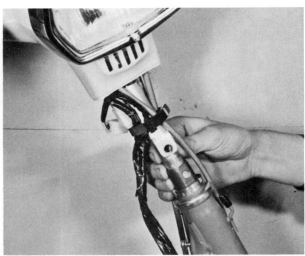

3.3e The handlebar assembly can now be displaced

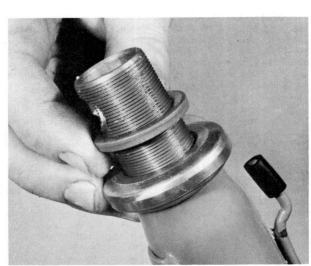

3.5a Remove the steering stem nuts, spacer ...

3.5b ... and upper bearing cone ...

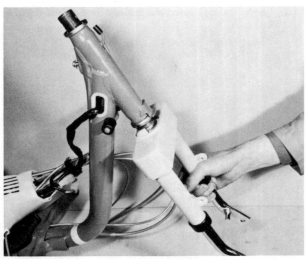

3.5c ... to permit removal of fork assembly

3.6 Bearing balls can be held in place with grease

3.7 Steering head bearings must be correctly adjusted

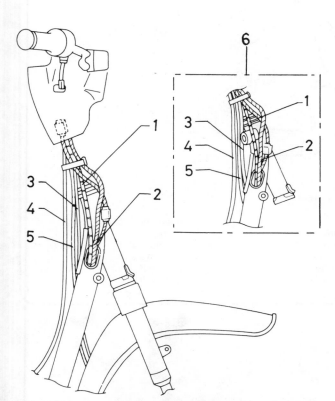

Fig. 4.2 Routing of steering head assembly control cables

1	Throttle cable	5	Front brake cable
2	Wiring harness	6	Models fitted with
3	Speedometer cable		steering lock
4	Rear brake cable		

4 Front forks: dismantling, examination and renovation

1   The procedure described below gives the method for overhauling the front forks once they have been removed from the machine as described in Section 3. It should be noted that a similar procedure can be applied when the forks are still in position in the steering head, in which case the front wheel must be removed and the machine supported to raise the front end prior to any dismantling work. Again, details will be found in Section 3.

2   Each of the lower fork legs is retained by a large internal circlip, and before any attempt is made to remove this it should be noted that the assembly is under moderate spring pressure. It was found to be convenient to compress the fork spring somewhat, holding it in position with a length of stout wire between the wheel spindle hole and the carrier bracket (see photograph).

3   With the fork leg suitably compressed, slide down the dust seal to expose the circlip which can be released with the aid of a substantial pair of circlip pliers. The wire can now be released and the lower leg assembly withdrawn from the fork tube.

4   The fork components should be laid out for examination, noting that the conical rubber bump stop is fitted inside the spring of the left-hand fork leg only. Wipe off any excess grease and check the lower leg assembly for signs of wear or damage. If this is discovered little can be done to repair it, the lower leg being a sealed unit with no replacement parts available. If there is noticeable free play between the lower leg and fork tube it will be necessary to renew one or both components. Before condemning the fork, take it to a Yamaha Service Agent who will be able to judge its condition by comparison with a new assembly, and can advise whether renewal is required.

5   Before reassembling the fork clean and degrease the lower leg assembly and the inside of the fork tube. The lower leg components should be given a generous coating of general purpose grease. Reassembly is now a reversal of the dismantling sequence.

5 Frame : examination and renovation

1   The frame is unlikely to require attention unless it is damaged as the result of an accident. In many cases, replacement of the frame is the only satisfactory course of action, if it is badly out of alignment. Comparatively few frame repair specialists have the necessary mandrels and jigs essential for the accurate re-setting of the frame and, even then, there is no means of assessing to what extent the frame may have been overstressed such that a later fatigue failure may occur.

2   After a machine has covered an extensive mileage, it is advisable to keep a close watch for signs of cracking or splitting at any of the welded joints. Rust can cause weakness at these joints particularly if they are unpainted. Minor repairs can be effected by welding or brazing, depending on the extent of the damage found.

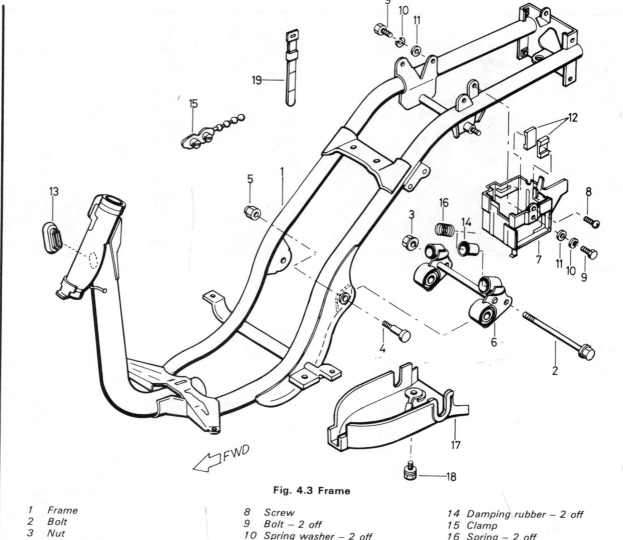

Fig. 4.3 Frame

1 Frame	8 Screw	14 Damping rubber – 2 off
2 Bolt	9 Bolt – 2 off	15 Clamp
3 Nut	10 Spring washer – 2 off	16 Spring – 2 off
4 Bolt – 2 off	11 Washer – 2 off	17 Engine guard
5 Nut – 2 off	12 Battery carrier pads	18 Bolt and washer
6 Engine mounting bracket	13 Cable grommet	19 Cable tie
7 Battery carrier		

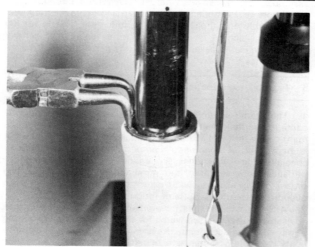

4.2 Use wire loop to compress spring during circlip removal

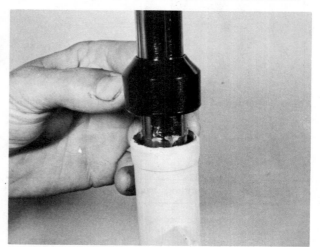

4.3a Displace dust seal and remove circlip ...

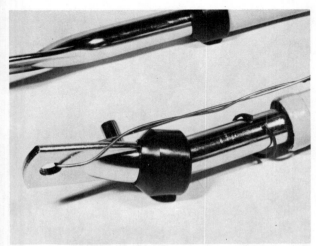

4.3b ... then free retaining wire

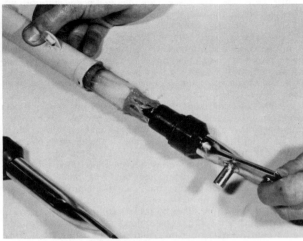

4.3c Fork leg components can be removed and cleaned

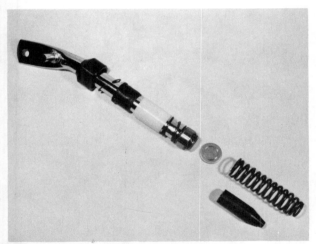

4.4a The fork leg assembly

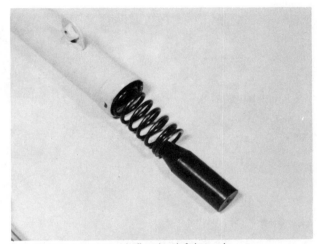

4.4b Rubber bump stop is fitted to left leg only

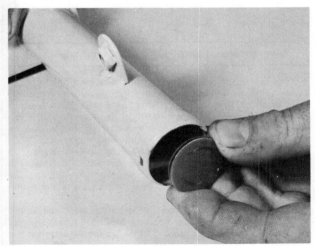

4.4c Do not omit to fit the spring seat

6 Rear suspension pivot: examination and renovation

1   As has already been mentioned, rear suspension is provided by arranging the engine/transmission unit so that it is free to pivot around its front mounting point, the rear of the assembly being controlled by a single coil spring and shock absorber unit. The front of the crankcase casting terminates in two large lugs in which are housed large sealed bearings. The bearings carry a transverse pivot tube which is located by means of circlips. A pivot bolt passes through this and the lugs of the engine mounting. This later item is itself free to pivot in relation to the frame, movement being controlled by two small compression springs. This system allows engine vibration to be absorbed by the springs instead of being transmitted to the frame and thus to the rider.

2   The front mounting components are, for all practical purposes, inaccessible until the engine/transmission unit has been removed from the frame, making maintenance impracticable. Fortunately the large pivot bearings are well lubricated during manufacture and should not require attention before a major engine overhaul is necessary. Should wear have developed in the bearings it will be detected as side-to-side movement of the engine/transmission unit. This can be checked by grasping the rear of the transmission casing and pushing it

from side to side. Any discernible play will necessitate prompt attention before the resulting poor handling causes an accident. It will be necessary to remove the engine/transmission assembly as described in Chapter 1, Section 4. It should be noted that it is possible to attend to the pivot area without the engine being removed completely, but it will be necessary to arrange some method of supporting the frame clear of the engine unit. Removal of the surrounding panels will be necessary in either case.

3   With the unit separated from the frame and on the workbench, release one of the pivot tube circlips which will be found against the inner face of each bearing. Move the circlip to the centre of the tube, which can then be displaced to one side. Remove both circlips from the exposed end of the tube and slide the latter clear of the bearings. The bearings themselves can now be removed by heating the lugs with boiling water to expand the alloy and pushing the bearings inwards. If necessary a large socket can be used as a drift during bearing removal. New bearings can be fitted by reversing the above sequences.

4   If necessary the engine mounting can be removed from the frame after releasing the nuts and pins which locate it. Take care not to lose the small compression springs which support it. The small damper cups which surround the springs should be renewed if worn or damaged, but little else will require attention.

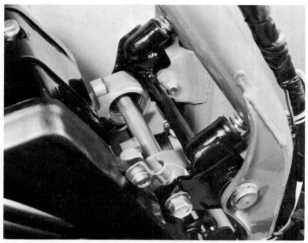
6.1a The engine pivot and mounting assembly

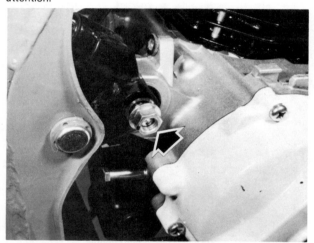
6.1b Free the engine unit by releasing pivot bolt

6.3a Slide circlips inwards to free pivot tube

6.3b Bearings can be removed by driving them inwards

7   Rear suspension unit: removal and replacement

1   The rear suspension unit consists of a coil spring surrounding a sealed, hydraulically damped shock absorber. No adjustment or dismantling of the unit is possible, and in the event of failure a new unit must be fitted. If problems do occur it will normally be due to seal failure in the damper unit which will result in a very harsh ride, and is potentially dangerous.

2   When removing the suspension unit it will be necessary to contrive some method of supporting the rear of the machine whilst the unit is not doing so. The easiest method is to place a suitable wooden wedge between the frame and the transmission casing.

3   The suspension unit can be removed after the upper mounting nut and the lower mounting bolt have been released. When refitting the unit note the following torque settings.

Rear suspension mounting torque settings
Upper   *2.3 kgf m (16.6 lbf ft)*
Lower   *1.8 kgf m (13.0 lbf ft)*

7.3a The rear suspension unit upper mounting

7.3b The rear suspension unit lower mounting

8 Centre stand: examination and maintenance

1 The Passola is equipped with a tubular steel centre stand which is mounted on the underside of the engine transmission unit. The stand pivots on a steel shaft which is retained at its plain end by a plain washer and an R-pin. A heavy extension spring retracts the stand when it is not in use. The condition of the spring and the pivot should be checked periodically and both should be kept clean and well lubricated.

2 Should the stand require attention, it may be removed by releasing the R-pin and washer and displacing the pivot shaft. Note that replacement can prove rather arduous because it is necessary to manoeuvre the stand into position against spring pressure whilst the pivot pin is fitted. There is no easy way of accomplishing this operation, and a mixture of patience and strength is essential. It is almost indispensable to have some assistance during reassembly.

9 Footboard and bodywork: maintenance

1 The Passola features weather protection of the type normally found on scooters, the major working parts being covered by an arrangement of plastic guards and covers, whilst the front of the machine is fitted with a footboard and legshields. The plastic parts do not require any special attention other than to avoid scratching when the machine is being cleaned.

2 The footboard is of pressed steel construction and this can be prone to rusting in time if not kept clean and free from road salt. It is well worth making sure that the underside of the footboard is clean, particularly in the vicinity of the outrigger supports to which it is bolted. The captive nuts are exposed to much of the dirt and water flung up by the front wheel and will rust up if not kept well lubricated.

10 Speedometer drive and cable: examination

1 Drive from the speedometer drive gearbox is transmitted to the instrument head by way of a flexible cable. This flexible cable consists of a resilient but torsionally rigid inner cable which runs inside, and is protected by, a reinforced outer cable. This arrangement allows the drive to pass through gentle bends and absorbs the relative movement between the front wheel and the instrument.

2 Although considered to be flexible, it is preferable to ensure that the cable does not pass through acute bends, which would shorten its effective life. The straighter the cable's run, the lower the rate of wear and risk of breakage.

3 If the speedometer ceases to function, suspect a broken cable. Inspection will show whether the inner cable has broken:

4 Spin the inner cable to check for resistance. Most cables have a tight spot, but if the resistance is severe and a wavering speedometer has been noted, the cable should be renewed. Lubrication is difficult with this type of cable, but an aerosol chain grease or a silicone-based lubricant can often be introduced using the aerosol's thin extension nozzle.

5 Drive to the cable takes the form of a gear mechanism built into the front brake backplate. This is not normally prone to wear, and maintenance can be restricted to inspection and re-greasing whenever the front brake components receive attention. Any mechanical failure will be obvious and will require renewal of the damaged parts.

11 Speedometer head: removal and refitting

1 The instrument head itself is generally reliable, and is the least likely culprit in the event of failure, this normally being attributable to the cable rather than the instrument mechanism. If, however, it is noted that the speedometer has ceased to function whilst the odometer (mileage recorder) still functions, the instrument can be assumed to have failed. No form of repair is practicable at home, and a new replacement speedometer will be required. The only alternative is to seek the assistance of one of the companies who specialise in this type of repair work.

2 To gain access to the speedometer head, start by releasing the two screws which retain the headlamp assembly to the handlebar cowling, these being located on its underside. Swing the lower edge of the headlamp clear of the cowling, then disengage the locating tang on its upper edge. The multi-pin connector can now be separated and the unit placed to one side.

3 Remove the two screws which pass up into the cowling from the underside, and then release the single rear screw to allow the upper section of the handlebar cowling to be lifted clear. Before the cowling can be separated it will be necessary to release the speedometer drive cable by unscrewing its retaining ring and to separate the wiring connectors from the ignition switch, warning lamps and the indicator relay.

4 Place the assembly on the workbench and start dismantling by removing the indicator relay from its rubber holder. The ignition switch should be removed next by releasing its retaining ring. Next, release the single screw which secures the steel backing plate to the speedometer. The plate can be removed and the speedometer head displaced from the cowling. Reassembly is a straightforward reversal of the dismantling sequence.

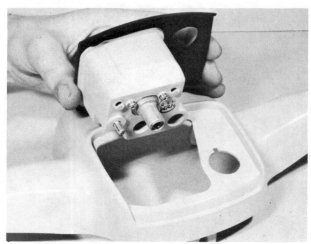

11.4 Speedometer and surround are removed as shown

12 Cleaning the machine: general

1   After removing all surface dirt with a rag or sponge washed frequently in clean water, the machine should be allowed to dry thoroughly. Application of car polish or wax to the cycle parts will give a good finish, particularly if the machine has been neglected for long period. Particular care must be taken to avoid scratching the numerous plastic panels on the machine. These are easily damaged if the accumulated road grime is not removed carefully using copious amounts of water.

2   The plated parts of the machine should require only a wipe with a damp rag. If the plated parts are badly corroded, as may occur during the winter wen the roads are salted, it is preferable to use one of the proprietary chrome cleaners. These often have an oily base, which will help to prevent the corrosion from recurring.

3   If the engine parts are particularly oily, use a cleaning compound such as 'Gunk' or 'Jizer'. Apply the compound whilst the parts are dry and work it in with a brush so that it has the opportunity to penetrate the film of grease and oil. Finish off by washing down liberally with plenty of water, taking care that it does not enter the carburettor or the electrics.

4   Whenever possible, the machine should be wiped down after it has been used in the wet, so that it is not garaged under

damp conditions which will promote rusting. Remember there is little chance of water entering the control cables and causing stiffness of operation if they are lubricated regularly as recommended in the Routine Maintenance Section.

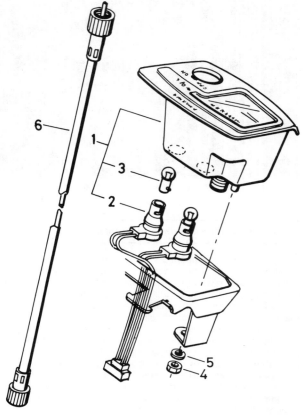

Fig. 4.4 Speedometer

1 Speedometer	4 Nut
assembly	5 Spring washer
2 Bulb holder – 2 off	6 Speedometer cable
3 Bulb – 2 off	

13 Fault diagnosis : frame and forks

Symptom	Cause	Remedy
Machine veers to left or right with hands off handlebars	Incorrect wheel alignment	Check and re-align.
	Bent forks	Check and renew.
	Twisted frame	Check and renew.
Machine rolls at low speeds	Overtight steering head bearings	Slacken and re-test
Machine judders when front brake is applied	Slack steering head bearings	Tighten until all play is taken up.
	Warped brake drum	Refer to Chapter 5.
Machine pitches badly on uneven surfaces	Ineffective forks	Check and renew.
	Ineffective rear suspension units	Check and renew.
Fork action stiff	Fork legs dirty or dry	Dismantle, clean and lubricate.
Machine wanders. Steering imprecise, rear wheel tends to hop	Worn swinging arm pivot	Dismantle and renew bearings and pivot shaft.

Chapter 5 Wheels, brakes and tyres

Contents

Specifications

Wheels

Type	Pressed steel type

Tyres

Size (front and rear)	2.75 x 10 – 4PR
Pressures:	
front	18 psi (1.25 kg cm^2)
rear	25 psi (1.75 kg cm^2)

Brakes

	Front	Rear
Type	Single leading shoe (sls) drum brake	
Drum diameter	80 mm (3.1496 in)	90 mm (3.5433 in)
Shoe diameter	80 mm (3.1496 in)	90 mm (3.5433 in)
Lining width	17 mm (0.6693 in)	20 mm (0.7874 in)
Lining thickness	3.5 mm (0.1378 in)	3.5 mm (0.1378 in)
Service limit	2.0 mm (0.0784 in)	2.0 mm (0.0784 in)
Return spring free length	44.5 mm (1.752 in)	32.7 mm (1.287 in)
Service limit	45.5 mm (1.791 in)	33.7 mm (1.327 in)

Torque settings

	kgf m	lbf ft
Front wheel spindle nut	3.5	25.3
Rear stub axle nut	6.0	43.3

1 General description

The Passola employs small diameter painted steel wheels of the type normally associated with scooters. The wheels are of pressed steel construction with an integral brake drum and wheel centre welded to the rim. The front wheel is of normal motorcycle fitting with a wheel spindle passing through the fork ends, whilst the rear wheel has a splined boss which engages a corresponding spline on the output shaft or stub axle. Tyres are 2.75 x 10-4PR front and rear.

A simple single leading shoe (sls) drum brake is fitted to both wheels, the brakes being controlled by handlebar levers in a similar arrangement to that found on bicycles. Though similar in size and construction the wheels are not interchangeable.

2 Wheels: general maintenance

1   Unlike conventional wire-spoked wheels, those of the Passola do not require regular maintenance checks and adjustment. Whilst this minimises routine servicing work it does mean

that any irregularities caused by damage over rough ground or impact with curbstones will probably necessitate renewal of the affected wheel. When cleaning the machine, examine both wheels noting that any paint chips must be repainted quickly if rusting is to be avoided. Check each wheel after cleaning for signs of wear in the wheel bearings. Any such deterioration will be evident in the form of free play and is indicative of the need for prompt attention.

3 Front wheel: removal and refitting

1   Place the machine securely on its centre stand ensuring that there is no danger of its falling over. The position of the stand is such that it will be necessary to raise the wheel clear of the ground prior to removal. This is best accomplished by placing suitable wooden blocks beneath the footboard outriggers.

2   Free the speedometer drive cable by releasing the wire clip which retains it to the brake plate. The clip has two small tangs which should be squeezed together using pointed-nose pliers to allow it to be lifted from its locating groove. The cable can now be pulled clear. Slacken and remove the front brake cable

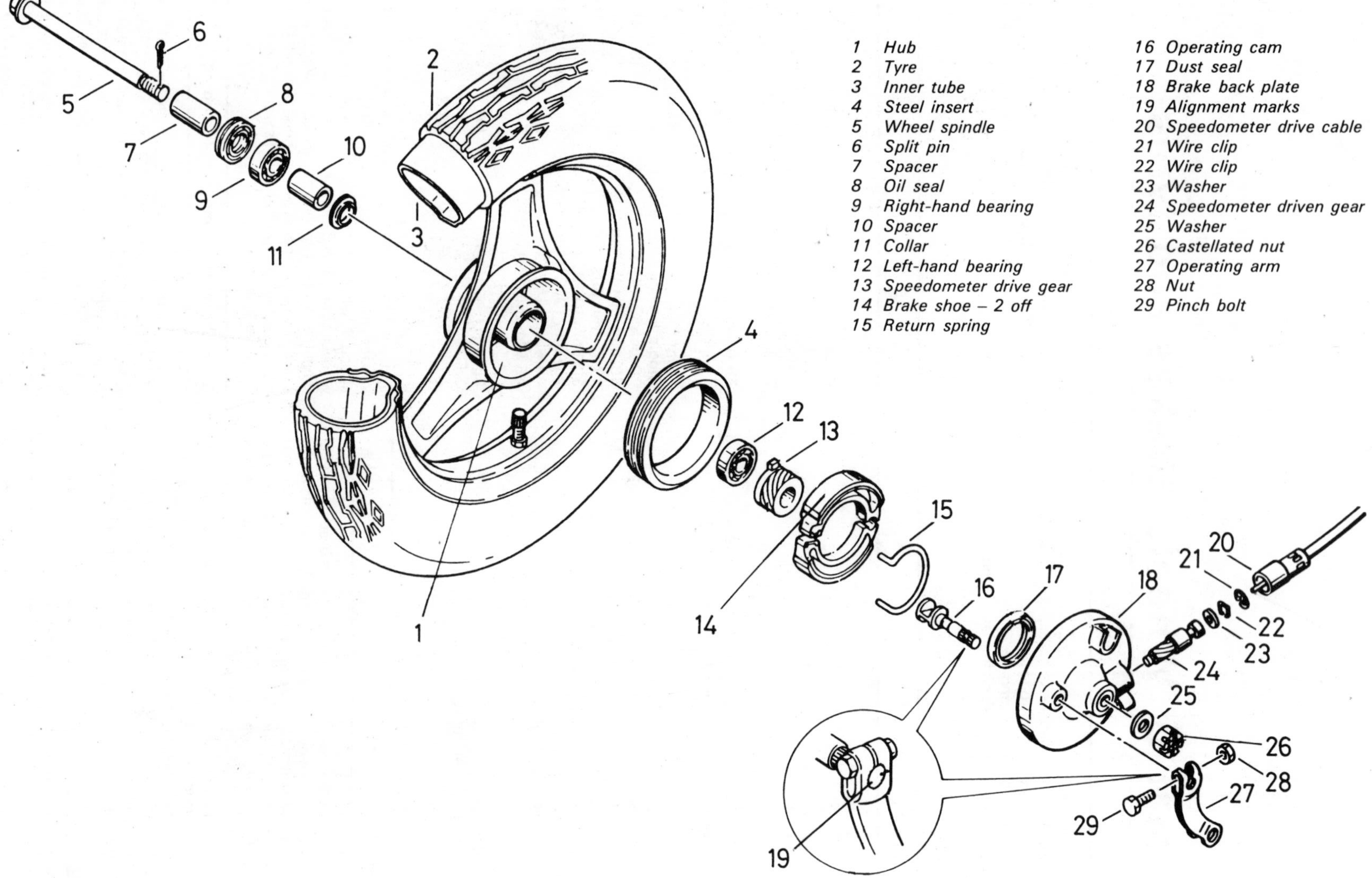

Fig. 5.1 Front wheel and brake assembly

1 Hub
2 Tyre
3 Inner tube
4 Steel insert
5 Wheel spindle
6 Split pin
7 Spacer
8 Oil seal
9 Right-hand bearing
10 Spacer
11 Collar
12 Left-hand bearing
13 Speedometer drive gear
14 Brake shoe – 2 off
15 Return spring
16 Operating cam
17 Dust seal
18 Brake back plate
19 Alignment marks
20 Speedometer drive cable
21 Wire clip
22 Wire clip
23 Washer
24 Speedometer driven gear
25 Washer
26 Castellated nut
27 Operating arm
28 Nut
29 Pinch bolt

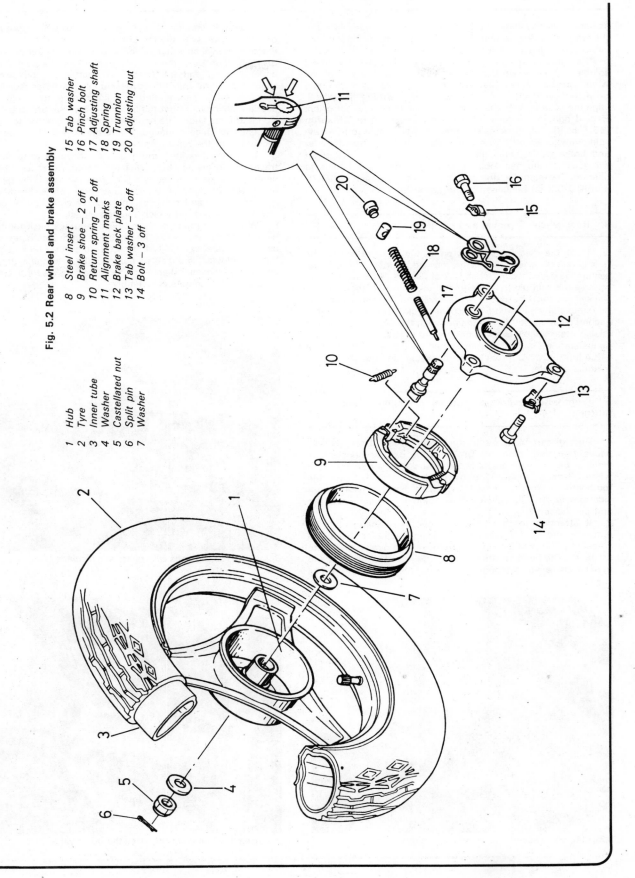

Fig. 5.2 Rear wheel and brake assembly

1 Hub
2 Tyre
3 Inner tube
4 Washer
5 Castellated nut
6 Split pin
7 Washer

8 Steel insert
9 Brake shoe – 2 off
10 Return spring – 2 off
11 Alignment marks
12 Brake back plate
13 Tab washer – 3 off
14 Bolt – 3 off

15 Tab washer
16 Pinch bolt
17 Adjusting shaft
18 Spring
19 Trunnion
20 Adjusting nut

adjuster and disengage the cable from the brake backplate and the brake arm. Reassemble the trunnion and the adjuster on the cable end to prevent their loss.

3   Straighten and remove the split pin which locates the wheel spindle nut, then remove the nut itself. Grasp the end of the wheel spindle and withdraw it to free the wheel which can then be manoeuvred clear of the forks. When refitting the wheel, wipe the spindle with a thin film of grease to prevent corrosion. Fit and tighten the castellated wheel spindle nut to 3.5 kgf m (25.3 lbf ft). Emergencies excepted, it is advisable to fit a new split pin whenever the wheel is removed. Refit the speedometer and brake cables, adjusting the latter to give a very slight clearance at the handlebar lever before the brake begins to operate. The manufacturer recommends a clearance of 10-20 mm (0.4-0.8 in) measured at the tip of the lever.

4   Rear wheel: removal and refitting

1   Place the machine securely on its centre stand so that the rear wheel is raised clear of the ground. Remove the exhaust system, as described in Section 12 of Chapter 2. Straighten and remove the split pin from the end of the stub axle, then remove the self-locking wheel nut and plain washer. The wheel can now be removed by pulling it off its splines. Take care not to lose the second plain washer which fits between the wheel hub and the casing. Reassembly is a straightforward reversal of the removal sequence, noting that the nut should be tightened to 6 kgf m (43.4 lbf ft). Do not forget to fit a new split pin through the hole in the stub axle.

5   Front wheel bearings: removal, examination and refitting

1   Any discernible play in the front wheel bearings will necessitate their renewal. The bearings can be checked by placing the machine on its centre stand and raising the front wheel clear of the ground by placing blocks beneath the footboard. Grasp the wheel firmly and attempt to rock it from side to side. Any clearance will be magnified at the wheel rim and can be felt.

2   If attention to the bearings proves necessary, start by removing the front wheel as detailed in Section 3. Place the wheel on the workbench and remove the brake backplate assembly. The bearings are a light interference fit in the hub and may be displaced by tapping them out with a small drift. It has

been found in practice that the best tool for this purpose is an old screwdriver with the top of the blade bent at a slight angle. Place the wheel on wooden blocks to provide clearance beneath the hub, then pass the drift down through the centre of the upper bearing and the spacer. The latter can be displaced slightly to allow the drift to bear upon the inner race of the lower bearing. Tap around the inner race to displace the bearing, taking care that the bearing is kept square to the bore. No great force should be required to remove it or the seal which precedes it. Once removed, invert the wheel and repeat the process with the remaining bearing.

3   Wash the bearings and hub in clean petrol to removal all traces of old grease. Be particularly careful to ensure that the bearings are kept spotlessly clean. When dry, spin the bearings and listen for signs of roughness as they rotate. Examine the bearing tracks and balls for any sign of corrosion or pitting, rejecting any bearing which seems suspect.

4   When fitting new or sound used bearings pack them with high melting-point grease. Fit the brake drum side bearing first, using a large socket as a drift so that the outer race takes the hammer blows. Fill the cavity between the bearings with grease and fit the spacer, then tap the remaining bearing and the grease seal to complete assembly.

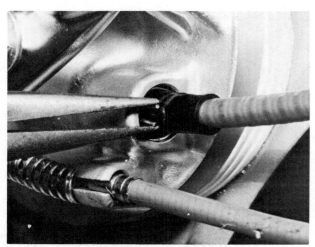

3.2a Grasp spring ends with pliers and displace clip ...

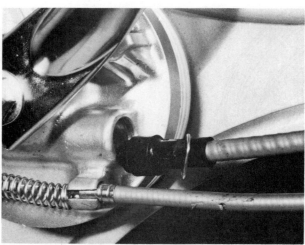

3.2b ... to allow speedometer cable to be removed

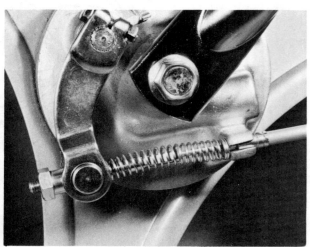

3.2c Remove adjuster nut to free the front brake cable

3.3a Extract split pin and remove nut

3.3b Displace the wheel spindle and remove spacer (arrowed) ...

3.3c ... and remove wheel. Note torque anchorage point (arrowed)

4.1 Rear wheel can be slid off after removal of single nut

5.4a Note the flanged spacer fitted between bearings

5.4b Pack wheel bearings with grease prior to installation

5.4c A hammer and large socket can be used to fit the bearings

5.4d The oil seal should be renewed as a precaution

6 Rear wheel bearings: general information

1   Unlike the front wheel, the rear wheel is not fitted with its own bearings. The hub is splined and fits directly on the rear stub axle, this being carried on bearings in the final drive casing. If play is detected it will be necessary to examine these bearings for wear or damage, and reference should be made to Chapter 1 for details. It should be noted that the rear wheel nut must be kept tight at all times. The split pin will prevent it and the wheel from falling off, but if it becomes slack play will develop between the splines of the wheel hub and the stub axle. Wear on these components will necessitate renewal of both.

7 Brakes: examination and renovation

1   Both wheels incorporate a single leading shoe (sls) drum brake, each of which is operated by a handlebar lever. Each of the brake cables terminates at the wheel end in a threaded rod. A nut is fitted on each to provide a means of adjustment to compensate for the gradual wear of the brake lining material. The brake plates incorporate a small curved scale adjacent to the brake cam end. A pointer is attached to the splined end of the cam and is designed to indicate the usable range of the lining material. When the pointer nears the limit mark it is necessary to dismantle and overhaul the brake.
2   To gain access to the brake it is first necessary to remove the appropriate wheel as described in Section 3 or 4 of this Chapter. In the case of the front wheel, the brake backplate assembly is removed with the wheel and can now be lifted clear. The rear brake backplate is mounted on the end of the final drive casing and can be removed after its three mounting bolts have been released. Note that these are retained by tab washers.
3   The brake drums should be checked for wear or damage after any accumulation of dust has been removed. It should be noted that this dust contains asbestos which can be harmful if inhaled. For this reason, **never** use compressed air to remove the dust. A petrol moistened rag will remove the dust and clean the drum surface quickly and safely. Look for signs of scoring or any other damage on the drum surface. If badly damaged it may be possible to have the drum skimmed in a lathe by a suitably-equipped specialist. Failing this, renewal of the entire wheel is inevitable. In practice, such damage is unlikely to be encoun-

tered, and very light scoring can be accepted. Any rusting of the drum surface may be removed by careful use of fine abrasive paper.
4   The shoes can be checked for wear by measuring the thickness of the lining material at the point where the greatest amount of wear has taken place. The nominal lining thickness is 3.5 mm (0.14 in), and the shoes must be renewed when they have worn down to 2.0 mm (0.08 in).
5   The front brake shoes can be removed once the return spring has been released. This takes the form of a large C-shaped spring ring, the ends of which engage in holes in the shoe ends. To release the shoes, grasp the ends furthest from the brake cam, pulling them apart and away from the backplate. The shoes can be allowed to fold inwards to help in freeing the brake cam ends.
6   The rear brake shoes have conventional extension coil springs fitted between the shoes. They can be freed by folding the shoes inwards until the ends can be disengaged from the cam and pivot. Once the shoes have been removed note the position of each spring in relation to the brake shoes before separating them.
7   If the existing shoes are to be refitted they should be wiped with a clean petrol-moistened rag to remove the accumulated brake dust. The rear shoes in particular should be examined for signs of oil contamination. If this is slight it may be possible to remove the oil with petrol. An aerosol solvent known as Utraclean, used mostly for electrical cleaning and degreasing, is ideal for this job and can be obtained from motor factors or through electrical shops. Severe contamination will necessitate renewal of the shoes. It follows that where oil contamination has been noted it will be necessary to rectify the leak before the brake is refitted. This is most likely to be a damaged oil seal on the stub axle and reference should be made to Chapter 1 for details.
8   Before refitting the brake shoes detach the brake cam operating arm by withdrawing the pinch bolt and push the camshaft from position. Clean thoroughly the shaft and the bore in the brake backplate through whih it passes. Grease the bearing surface of the camshaft before reinstalling it in the backplate. When fitting the operating arm note the punch marks on the arm boss and shaft end. These should be in alignment.
9   Reassembly of the brakes is a direct reversal of the removal sequence. Some care may be needed in fitting the shoes against return spring pressure. Make sure that the backplate is clean and apply a smear of grease to the brake cam faces and pivot before the shoes are fitted. Do not forget to reset the brake adjustment when reassembly is complete.

Tyre removal: Deflate inner tube and insert lever in close proximity to tyre valve

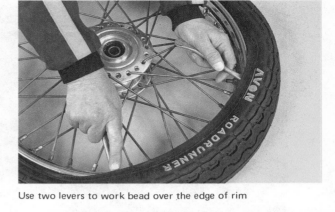

Use two levers to work bead over the edge of rim

When first bead is clear, remove tyre as shown

Tyre fitting: Inflate inner tube and insert in tyre

Lay tyre on rim and feed valve through hole in rim

Work first bead over rim, using lever in final section

Use similar technique for second bead, finish at tyre valve position

Push valve and tube up into tyre when fitting final section, to avoid trapping

7.1 Wear limit pointer is fitted behind the brake arm

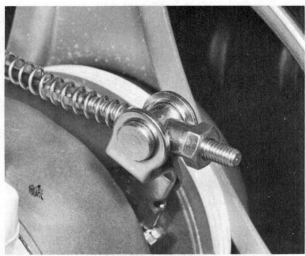

7.2a To remove rear brake backplate, free cable ...

7.2b ... and then remove mounting bolts (arrowed)

7.4 Measure lining thickness to determine the extent of wear

7.5 Front brake shoes are removed as shown

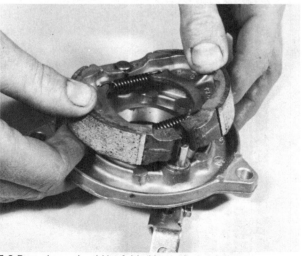

7.6 Rear shoes should be folded inwards to release

7.7a The front brake shoes and return spring

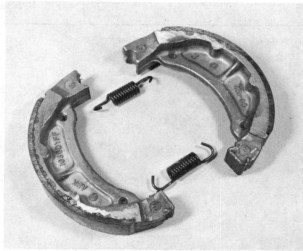

7.7b The rear brake shoes and return spring

7.8a Grease the brake cam during overhaul

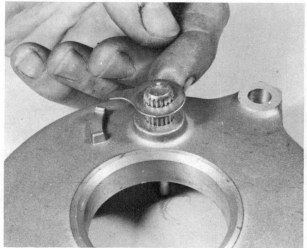

7.8b Refit wear indicator pointer as shown

7.8c Note index marks on brake arm and cam

7.8d Note tab washer which locks clamp bolt

7.8e Renew this seal if grease has entered brake

7.8f Plastic speedometer drive gear can be slid off its boss

7.8g Ensure that the speedometer gears are well greased

7.8h Ensure that the drive dogs engage when brake is refitted

8 Tyres: removal and refitting

1   At some time or other the need will arise to remove and replace the tyres, either as a result of a puncture or because a replacement is required to offset wear. To the inexperienced, tyre changing represents a formidable task, yet if a few simple rules are observed and the technique learned the whole operation is surprisingly simple.

2   To remove the tyre from either wheel, first detach the wheel from the machine by following the procedure in Section 2 of 4 depending on whether the front or the rear wheel is involved. Deflate the tyre by removing the valve insert and when it is fully deflated, push the bead of the tyre away from the wheel rim on both sides so that the bead enters the centre well of the rim. Remove the locking cap and push the tyre valve into the tyre itself.

3   Insert a tyre lever close to the valve and lever the edge of the tyre over the outside of the wheel rim. Very little force should be necessary; if resistance is encountered it is probably due to the fact that the tyre beads have not entered the well of the wheel rim all the way round the tyre.

4   Once the tyre has been edged over the wheel rim it is easy to work around the wheel rim so that the tyre is completely free on one side. At this stage, the inner tube can be removed.

5   Working from the other side of the wheel, ease the other edge of the tyre over the outside of the wheel rim that is furthest away. Continue to work around the rim until the tyre is free completely from the rim.

6   If a puncture has necessitated the removal of the tyre, reinflate the inner tube and immerse it in a bowl of water to trace the source of the leak. Mark its position and deflate the tube. Dry the tube and clean the area around the puncture with a petrol-soaked rag. When the surface has dried, apply the rubber solution and allow this to dry before removing the backing from the patch and applying the patch to the surface.

7   It is best to use a patch of the self-vulcanising type, which will form a very permanent repair. Note that it may be necessary to remove a protective covering from the top surface of the patch after is has sealed in position. Inner tubes made from synthetic rubber may require a special type of patch and adhesive, if a satisfactory bond is to be achieved.

8   Before replacing the tyre, check the inside to make sure the agent that caused the puncture is not trapped. Check also the outside of the tyre, particularly the tread area, to make sure nothing is trapped that may cause a further puncture. Check the well of the wheel for signs of rusting, a frequent cause of punctures with wheels of this type. If necessary, de-rust the wheel and re-paint it before the tyre is fitted.

9   If the inner tube has been patched on a number of past

occasions, or if there is a tear or large hole, it is preferable to discard it and fit a replacement. Sudden deflation may cause an accident.

10 To replace the tyre inflate the inner tube sufficiently for it to assume a circular shape but only just. Then push it into the tyre so that it is enclosed completely. Lay the tyre on the wheel at an angle and insert the valve through the rim tape and the hole in the wheel rim. Attach the locking cap on the first few threads, sufficient to hold the valve captive in its correct location.

11 Starting at the point furthest from the valve, push the tyre bead over the edge of the wheel rim until it is located in the central well. Continue to work around the tyre in this fashion until the whole of one side of the tyre is on the rim. It may be necessary to use a tyre lever during the final stages.

12 Make sure there is no pull on the tyre valve and again commencing with the area furthest from the valve, ease the other bead of the tyre over the edge of the rim. Finish with the area close to the valve, pushing the valve up into the tyre until the locking cap touches the rim. This will ensure the inner tube is not trapped when the last section of the bead is edged over the rim with a tyre lever.

13 Check that the inner tube is not trapped at any point. Reinflate the inner tube, and check that the tyre is seating correctly around the wheel rim. There should be a thin rib moulded around the wall of the tyre on both sides, which should be equidistant from the wheel rim at all points. If the tyre is unevenly located on the rim, try bouncing the wheel when the tyre is at the recommended pressure. It is probable that one of

the beads has not pulled clear of the centre well.

14 Always run the tyres at the recommended pressures and never under or over-inflate. The correct pressures for solo use are given in the Specifications Section of this Chapter. It should be remembered that the small size of the tyres means that the loss of a small quantity of air will result in a significant drop in pressure, so regular checks on tyre pressure should not be overlooked.

15 Tyre replacement is aided by dusting the side walls, particularly in the vicinity of the beads, with a liberal coating of French chalk. Washing-up liquid can also be used to good effect, but this has the disadvantage of causing the inner surfaces of the wheel to rust.

16 Never fit a tyre that has a damaged tread or side wall. Apart from the legal aspects, there is a very great risk of a blow-out which can have serious consequences on any two wheel vehicle.

17 Tyre valves rarely give trouble, but it is always advisable to check whether the valve itself is leaking before removing the tyre. Do not forget to fit the dust cap, which forms an effective second seal. The tyre valve dust cap is often left off when a tyre has been replaced, despite the fact the it serves an important two-fold function. Firstly, it prevents dirt or other foreign matter from entering the valve and causing the valve to stick open when the tyre pump is next applied. Secondly, it forms an effective second seal so that in the event of the tyre valve leaking, air will not be lost.

9 Fault diagnosis: wheels, brakes and tyres

Symptom	Cause	Remedy
Handlebars oscillate at low speeds	Buckle or flat in wheel rim, most probably front wheel Tyre not straight on rim	Check rim alignment by spinning wheel. Renew wheel if damaged. Check tyre alignment.
Machine lacks power and accelerates poorly	Brakes binding	Warm brake drums provide best evidence.
Brakes grab when applied gently	End of brake shoes not chamfered Elliptical brake drum	Chamfer with file. Lightly skim in lathe (specialist attention needed).
Brake pull-off sluggish	Brake cam binding in housing Weak brake shoe springs	Free and grease. Renew if springs not displaced.
Brakes ineffective	Contaminated or glazed linings	Remove and renew or remove glaze as necessary.
Brakes feel spongy	Cable badly routed Stretched brake operating cables	Re-route cable(s) avoiding sharp bends. Renew cables
Tyre wears more rapidly in middle of tread	Over inflation	Check pressures and run at recommended settings.
Tyres wear rapidly at outer edges of tread.	Under inflation	Ditto.

Chapter 6 Electrical system

For information and revisions to later models, see Chapter 7

Contents

Specifications

Electrical system

Type	Flywheel generator, battery/direct lighting
Voltage	6 volt
Earth	Negative

Charging system

	Day	Night
Output:		
At 3000 rpm	1.2A	0.55A
At 8000 rpm	2.5A	2.3A
Charging coil resistance	0.3 ohm ± 20%	
Lighting coil resistance	0.2 ohm ± 20%	
Lighting output	6.0 volt or more @ 3000 rpm	
	8.0 volt or less @ 8000 rpm	

Rectifier

Make	Stanley or Toshiba
Type	DE4504 or 55108
Capacity	4A
Maximum voltage	400V

Battery

6V 4Ah

Horn

Make	Nikko
Type	GF-6
Max. amperage	1.5A or less

Indicator relay

Model	FR-9TO6
Type	Hot wire
Frequency	90 c.p.m
Capacity	8W x 2 + 0.3W

Fuse

10A

Bulbs

Headlamp	6 volt 25/25W
Tail lamp	6 volt 5/21W
Indicators	6 volt 8W
Oil level warning	6 volt 3W
Speedometer light	6 volt 3W

1 General description

The Passola features a 6 volt electrical system powered by a crankshaft mounted flywheel generator. Alternating current (ac) is fed to a rectifier where it is converted to direct current (dc) for battery charging purposes. A 6 volt 4 Ah battery is fitted, the parking and instrument lights, indicators, horn and brake lights being powered from this side of the system. The headlamp is powered directly from the flywheel generator.

2 Charging system: checking the output

1   The charging system output can be tested using a multimeter set on the 0 - 10 amp current scale. Note that some of the cheaper multimeters are only capable of measuring milliamps, and are not suitable for this purpose. Remove the rear cowl to gain access to the battery and disconnect the battery positive (+) lead. Attach the negative probe lead from the multimeter or ammeter to the battery positive terminal, and the positive probe lead to the battery positive lead.
2   Start the engine and check the ammeter readings comparing them with the figures shown in the table below. Unless a tachometer is available the engine speed must be estimated, but this should suffice to give an impression of the charging system condition. It must be remembered that the transmission will be engaged as the engine speed increases, so make quite sure that the rear wheel is clear of the ground and that there is no risk of the machine rolling off its stand.

Charging system output test
UK models
Lights off   1.2A @ 3000 rpm
                  2.5A @ 8000 rpm
Lights on   0.55A @ 3000 rpm
                  2.3A @ 8000 rpm

Other models (Denmark, Finland)
Lights off   0.1A @ 3000 rpm
                  3.3A ± 0.7A @ 8000 rpm
Lights on   0.1A @ 3000 rpm
                  1.7A ± 0.7A @ 8000 rpm

3   If the readings obtained are substantially different from those shown above, check the lighting coil resistance and rectifier condition as described in the following Sections.

3 Flywheel generator: checking the lighting coil resistance

1   If the operation of the flywheel generator is suspect, the resistance of the lighting coil should be measured using a multimeter capable of measuring ohms (not kilo ohms) as described below. Trace the generator output leads back to the connector block next to the air filter. Separate the connector and measure the resistance between the various leads according to the following figures.

Lighting/charging coil resistance test
UK models
White to earth   0.3 ohms ± 20%
Yellow to earth   0.2 ohms ± 20%

Other models (Denmark, Finland)
Green/red to earth   0.3 ohms ± 10%
Yellow to earth   0.27 ohms ± 10%
Green to earth   0.25 ohms ± 10%

2   If the readings obtained conflict with those shown above it is likely that the lighting coil is faulty. Have the condition of the flywheel generator tested by a Yamaha Service Agent who will be able to advise whether renewal is necessary.

4 Rectifier: testing

1   The rectifier is a small encapsulated diode bolted to the rear of the battery tray. Its purpose is to convert the ac output of the flywheel generator into dc to charge the battery. It does this by blocking half of the output wave from the generator. Its operation is analogous to that of a one way valve in that it will allow the current to flow in one direction only, and this function can be checked by measuring its resistance with a multimeter set on the ohms scale.
2   Disconnect the rectifier leads and attach one probe lead from the multimeter to each of the two terminals. Note the reading obtained, then reverse the probe leads and check the reading once more. If the rectifier is functioning normally it should allow current to pass in one direction but not in the other, thus a reading of no resistance should be shown, with infinite resistance when the probes are reversed. If the readings obtained do not correspond, the unit is faulty and must be renewed.

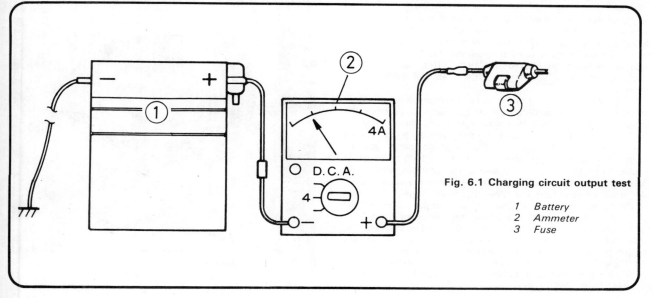

Fig. 6.1 Charging circuit output test

1   Battery
2   Ammeter
3   Fuse

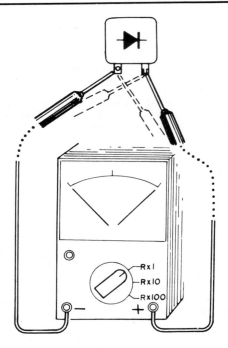

Fig. 6.2 Rectifier test

5   Lighting circuit: fault finding

Bulb failure

1   Referring to the appropriate Section in this Chapter, remove the defective bulb and examine it carefully, it is normally possible to establish the nature of the fault by checking the appearance of the bulb. If the element is broken, but appears bright and clean, it is probable that the failure was a result of a mechanical fault; that is, the element has merely fractured due to faulty manufacture and/or vibration. A fused bulb, on the other hand, will have a vastly different appearance. The element will have melted, and in extreme cases will have vapourised and blackened the glass envelope, sometimes to the extent that the glass surface becomes opaque, or even silvered. This type of failure is due to electrical overload, as opposed to vibration damage.

2   It is not uncommon, with direct lighting systems, for the whole complement of bulbs to appear to fail simultaneously. What actually happens is that one of the bulbs breaks or fuses, and this subjects the remainder to a sudden surge of power, and this surge fuses the rest of the bulbs. This type of failure normally occurs at high engine speeds, and for the following reason.

3   The combined rating of the bulbs is chosen at manufacture to match the average output of the generator. In practice, the output varies according to engine speed, and this is why the lights dim at tickover, and brighten progressively as the engine speed rises. At peak revs, the bulbs are at maximum capacity, and it is under these circumstances that one bulb may fuse or break. This passes the extra power to the remaining bulbs, and can set up a chain reaction, fusing the entire complement.

4   It will be seen from the above that any change in the rating of the bulbs will affect the system overall. In particular, the use of a bulb of higher wattage than normal will cause a reduction in light output in the whole system, and should be avoided. The fitting of a bulb of lower wattage will cause the overall light output to rise, but will make the system more prone to failure. To this end, it is important to ensure that any replacement bulb is of the correct rating. In the event of a blown bulb, check the system as described below.

Wiring failure

5   From the beginning it will be noted that the interruption of the circuit by a bulb failure will overload the remainder, and a similar situatiion will arise if the supply to a bulb is interrupted or if the earth return is erratic. In practice, this condition causes the majority of bulb failures. If bulb failures become persistent, the various wiring connections must be checked very carefully. All terminals and connectors should be cleaned and checked for tightness, not forgetting the earth connections to the frame. The various contact faces in bullet connectors must be kept clean, and should be burnished with abrasive paper to ensure a sound connection is made.

6   Do not omit to check the handlebar switch unit for continuity using a multimeter set to the resistance function. In winter, the system will benefit greatly if protected by one of the numerous silicone-based maintenance sprays, such as WD 40, Plus Gas or similar.

7   Finally, it is a sound precaution to invest in a set of replacement bulbs which should be carried on the machine to cater for emergencies.

6   Headlamp: adjustment and bulb renewal

1   The headlamp is mounted in the front of the moulded plastic handlebar nacelle. The vertical alignment can be set by means of the single central screw on the edge of the headlamp rim. In most countries there are laws which regulate the height at which the headlamp beam is set. In the UK, the regulations stipulate that the lighting system must be arranged so that the light will not dazzle a person standing in the same horizontal plane as the vehicle at a distance greater than 25 feet from the lamp, whose eye level is not less than 3 feet 6 inches above that plane. It is easy to approximate this setting by placing the machine 25 feet away from a wall, on a level road, and setting the dip beam height so that it is concentrated at the same height as the distance from the centre of the headlamp to the ground.

2   In the event of bulb failure, the headlamp lens and reflector assembly can be released from the nacelle after the two screws which pass through the underside of the rim have been released. Pull the bottom of the unit outwards, then unhook the tang at the top of the nacelle to free the unit.

3   The headlamp bulb holder is a bayonet fit in the recess in the reflector. To release the holder, push it inwards slightly and rotate it to the left. The bulb is a push fit in the reflector and may be lifted out after releasing the holder. Note that the bulb is so constructed that it may be fitted in one position only.

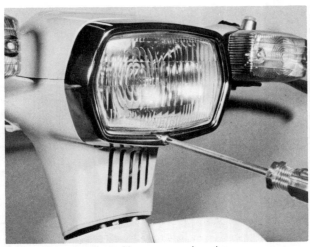

6.1 Headlamp is adjusted by screw on rim edge

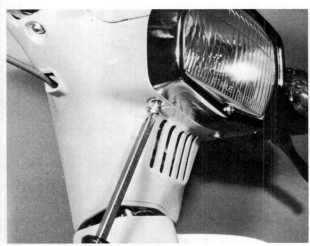

6.2 Two screws secure headlamp to nacelle

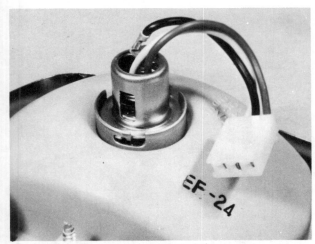

6.3a Bulbholder can be removed by twisting ...

6.3b ... to allow bulb to be removed

7 Tail lamp: bulb renewal

1 The moulded plastic cover of the rear lamp is retained by two screws. When these screws are removed, the cover can be removed and the bulb exposed.
2 The bulb is of the bayonet type and can be removed by pushing it upwards, and turning it anticlockwise. Ensure that the replacement bulb is of the appropriate wattage.
3 Consistent problems with bulbs blowing may be traced to a faulty earth or feed connection. Keep the main connections bright by cleaning with fine emery strip.
4 Take care not to overtighten the two cover retaining screws when refitting the cover as it is very easy to crack the plastic moulding.

8 Indicators: bulb renewal

1 The indicator lenses are each retained by two screws and are easily removed to give access to the bulbs. The bulbs are single filimant bayonet cap fitting and can be removed by pushing them inwards and turning them anticlockwise. When fitting new bulbs, ensure that they are of similar rating to the old items.

9 Indicator relay: location and renewal

1 The indicator relay is located inside the headlamp nacelle, access to it being gained by releasing the headlamp lens and reflector assembly. The relay is a cylindrical component held by a rubber mounting to the underside of the speedometer bracket.
2 If the flasher unit is functioning correctly, a series of audible clicks will be heard when the indicator lamps are in action. If the unit malfunctions and all the bulbs are in working order, the usual symptom is one initial flash before the unit goes dead; it will be encessary to replace the unit complete if the fault cannot be attributed to any other cause.
3 Take great care when handling the unit because it is easily damaged if dropped.

10 Headlamp nacelle: separation for access to electrical components

1 To gain full access to the horn, speedometer, warning lamps, flasher relay and ignition switch it may prove advantageous to remove the upper half of the headlamp nacelle. Start by removing the headlamp as described in Section 6 paragraph 2.
2 The upper section is secured by two screws which pass up into it from the underside, plus a single screw at the rear. With these removed, lift the section sufficiently to allow the speedometer cable to be released. Disconnect the ignition switch, indicator relay and warning lamp leads, and lift the nacelle clear.

11 Instrument panel bulbs: removal

1 The speedometer houses two bulbs carried in rubber bulbholders which are a push fit in the back of the housing. The two lamps can be identified by the colours of the leads running to them. The lamp with the blue/white and black leads is the speedometer illumination lamp, whilst the oil level warning lamp has a grey and a black lead. Note the position of each prior to removal to avoid any confusion that might arise during removal.

2   The bulbs are a bayonet fit in the holders and should be replaced by bulbs of similar wattage when renewal is required, both being 6 volt 3W. Check that the bulbholders locate correctly and that they have not become interchanged.

12 Horn: location and examination

1   The horn is mounted inside the headlamp nacelle access to it being gained after the top section of the nacelle has been removed as described in Section 10. The horn is well protected in the nacelle, and will not normally require attention. It is a sealed unit and cannot be dismantled for full examination or repair, a new unit being the only option. Before condemning the horn, check that the wiring and horn button are working properly.

8.1a Remove the two lens screws to free lens

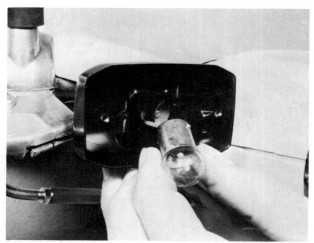

8.1b Bulb is a bayonet fitting

Fig. 6.3 Headlamp

1	Headlamp assembly	6	Beam height adjusting
2	Bulb		screw
3	Bulb holder	7	Spring
4	Reflector	8	Retaining spring clip
5	Rim	9	Screw/washer – 2 off

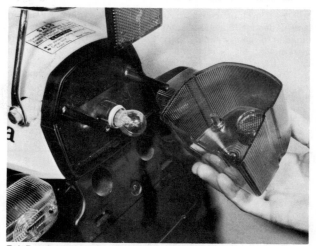

7.1 Rearlamp lens is removed to reveal bulb

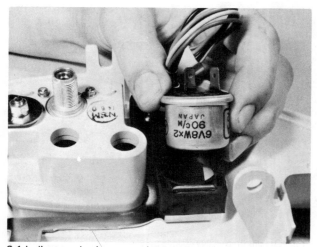

9.1 Indicator relay is mounted next to speedometer

10.1a Remove two screws on underside of nacelle ...

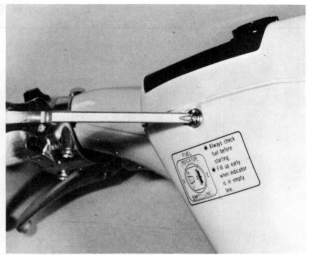

10.1b ... and single screw at rear

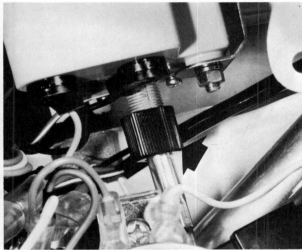

10.1c Release cable by unscrewing knurled ring (arrowed)

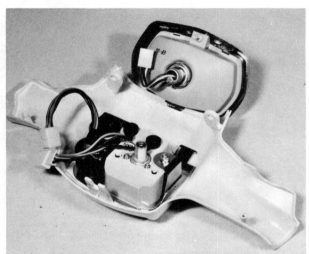

10.1d Upper section can now be removed as shown

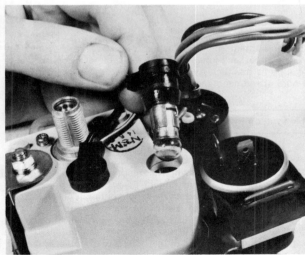

11.1 Instrument and warning bulbs are push fit

12.1 Horn is mounted in base of nacelle

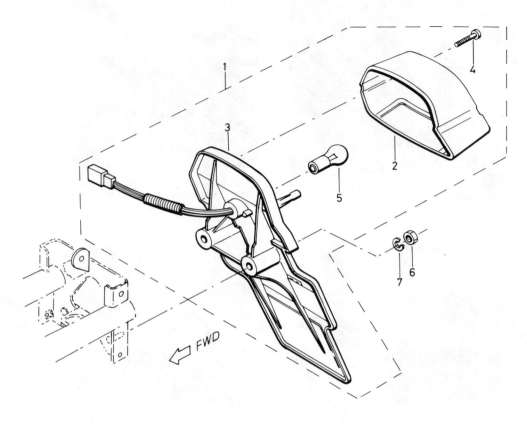

Fig. 6.4 Tail lamp

1 *Tail lamp assembly*	3 *Mounting bracket*	5 *Bulb*	7 *Washer – 2 off*
2 *Lens*	4 *Screw – 2 off*	6 *Nut – 2 off*	

13 Stop lamp switches: location and examination

1   A small plunger-type switch is built into each of the brake levers and these serve to operate the brake lamp when either brake is operated. The switches rarely give rise to problems, but can be kept in good condition by spraying them with WD40 or similar when carrying out general maintenance and lubrication jobs. The switches are a push fit in the lever stock, and must be renewed if they fail to operate. No repair is practicable.

14 Wiring: layout and examination

1   The wiring harness is colour-coded and will correspond with the accompanying wiring diagram. Where socket connectors are used, they are designed so that reconnection can be made in the correct position only.

2   Visual inspection will show whether there are no breaks or frayed outer coverings which will give rise to short circuits. Another source of trouble may be the snap connectors and sockets, where the connector has not been pushed fully home in the outer housing.

3   Intermittent short circuits can often be traced to a chafed wire that passes through or is close to a metal component such as a frame member. Avoid tight bends in the lead or situations where a lead can become trapped between casings.

15 Ignition switch: removal and testing

1   Access to the ignition switch is gained by removing the upper section of the headlamp nacelle as described in Section 10 of this Chapter. The switch is secured by a large knurled ring on the outside of the instrument panel. The operation of the switch can be checked by testing continuity between the various leads with the switch in its different settings. A multimeter set on the resistance scale will indicate whether continuity exists. The various conections can be seen in the wiring diagram at the end of this book. For example, in the OFF position the Black and Black/red lead should be connected, and the remainder insulated. If the switch proves to be defective, a new unit must be fitted. It is not practible to dismantle or repair the switch unit.

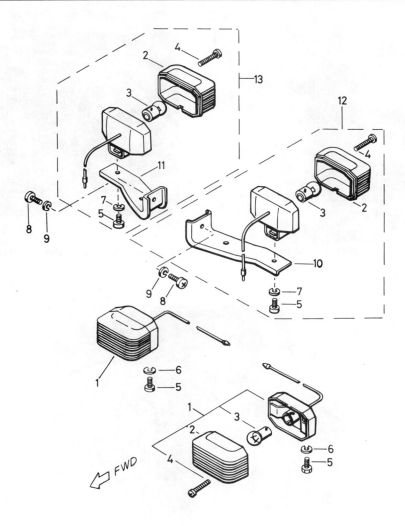

Fig. 6.5 Indicators

1	Front indicator assembly – 2 off	6	Washer – 2 off	10	Left-hand rear mounting bracket
2	Lens – 4 off	7	Spring washer – 2 off	11	Right-hand rear mounting bracket
3	Bulb – 4 off	8	Screw – 2 off	12	Left-hand rear indicator
4	Screw – 8 off	9	Spring washer – 2 off	13	Right-hand rear indicator
5	Screw – 4 off				

16 Fuse: location and renewal

1   The electrical system is protected by a single 10A fuse fitted to an in-line holder in the battery positive (+) lead. In the event of a short circuit the fuse will melt, or 'blow', thus preventing damage to the rest of the system by isolating it. It is important to establish the cause of the failure before the new fuse is fitted, though on occasions a simple current surge will have caused the problem.

2   The fuse holder contains a spare fuse of the appropriate rating, and this must be replaced as soon as possible if it has been used. In an emergency it is possible to wrap some aluminium foil around a blown fuse, purely as a get-you-home method. It should be noted, however, that this will leave the electrical system unprotected, so it is vital that the fault which caused the fuse to blow is eliminated first, and that a new fuse is fitted as soon as possible.

17 Battery: charging procedure

1   The normal charging rate for the 4 amp hour battery is 0.4 amps. A more rapid charge, not exceeding 1 amp cam be given in an emergency. The higher charge should, if possible, be avoided since it will shorten the working life of the battery.

2   Make sure that the battery charger connections are correct, red to positive and black to negative. It is preferable to remove the battery from the machine whilst it is being charged and to remove the vent plug from each cell. When the battery is reconnected to the machine, the black lead must be connected to the negative terminal and the red lead to positive. This is most important, as the machine has a negative earth system. If the terminals are inadvertently reversed, the electrical system will be damaged permanently. The rectifier will be destroyed by a reversal of the current flow.

15.1 The ignition switch can be removed as shown

16.1 Fuse holder also carries spare fuse

17.1 Check electrolyte level prior to charging

18 Fault diagnosis: electrical system

Symptom	Cause	Remedy
Complete electrical failure	Blown fuse	Locate fault and renew fuse
	Broken wire from generator	Reconnect
	Lighting switch faulty	Renew switch
	Generator not charging	Check output
Dim lights	Bad connections	Renovate, paying particular attention to earth connections
Constantly 'blowing' bulbs	Vibration	Check bulb holders are secure
	Poor earth connections	Renovate
Battery not charging	Damaged rectifier	Renew
	Short in charging/lighting coil	Renew stator assembly

Left-hand view of the SA50 ME model

Right-hand view of the SA50 ME model

Chapter 7 The 1982 to 1985 models

Contents

Specifications

The specifications shown below relate to the UK kickstart SA50 ME (13H) model, engine and frame number 2T4 260101 onwards, and to the UK electric start SA50 ME (13J) model, engine and frame number 2T4-270101 onwards. All specifications follow the sequence of the main text and appear only where they differ from those shown in the relevant Chapter.

Model dimensions and weight

Length .... 1570 mm (61.8 in)
Height .... 985 mm (38.7 in)

Specifications relating to Chapter 1

Engine
Compression ratio 6.0:1

Piston
Piston to bore clearance .... 0.034 – 0.047 mm (0.0013 – 0.0019 in)
Piston oversizes .... +0.25 mm (+0.01 in), +0.50 mm (+0.02 in), +0.75 mm (+0.03 in), +1.00 mm (+0.04 in)

Cylinder barrel
Taper limit .... 0.004 mm (0.0002 in)
Ovality limit .... 0.0025 mm (0.0001 in)

Crankshaft assembly
Big-end side clearance .... 0.25 – 0.45 mm (0.0098 – 0.0177 in)
Service limit .... not available
Deflection at small-end .... 0.4 – 0.8 mm (0.0157 – 0.0315 in)
Service limit .... not available

Clutch
Clutch spring free length .... 32 mm (1.26 in)

Torque wrench settings
Note: All fasteners listed as having a torque wrench setting of 1.0 kgf m (7.2 lbf ft) should be tightened to 0.9 kgf m (6.5 lbf ft).

Specifications relating to Chapter 2

Carburettor
Make .... Teikei Kikaki
Type Y12P
I.D. mark 5J3-00
Main jet 94
Main air jet 2.5
Jet needle 3R20
Needle clip position 3
Needle jet .... H80 [2.080]

Cutaway	....	2.0
Pilot jet	....	4.0
Pilot air screw (turns out)	....	$1\frac{3}{4}$
Starter jet	....	42
Float height	....	25 $\pm$ 1 mm (0.98 $\pm$ 0.04 in)
Idle speed	....	1700 rpm

Lubrication system

Pump colour code	....	Grey
Minimum stroke	....	0.35 – 0.40 mm (0.0138 – 0.0157 in)
Maximum stroke	....	1.05 – 1.20 mm (0.0413 – 0.0472 in)
Minimum output per 200 strokes	....	0.673 – 0.770 cc (0.0237 – 0.0272 Imp fl oz)
Maximum output per 200 strokes	....	2.020 – 2.309 cc (0.0712 – 0.0814 Imp fl oz)

Specifications relating to Chapter 3

Flywheel generator

Make	....	Yamaha
Model	....	F5J3
Voltage	....	6
Pulser coil resistance:		
kickstart models	....	20 ohm $\pm$ 10% @ 20°C (68°F)
electric start models	....	30 ohm $\pm$ 10% @ 20°C (68°F)
Source coil resistance:		
kickstart models	....	300 ohm $\pm$ 10% @ 20°C (68°F)
electric start models	....	380 ohm $\pm$ 10% @ 20°C (68°F)

CDI unit

Make	....	Yamaha
Type	....	5G3

Specifications relating to Chapter 4

Rear suspension

Rear wheel travel	....	53 mm (2.09 in)

Torque wrench settings

Component	kgf m	lbf ft
Handlebar retaining bolt	2.9	21.0
Steering stem locknut	3.0	22.0
Fuel tank mounting bolts	1.6	11.0

Specifications relating to Chapter 6

Charging system (electric start models)

	Day	Night
Output:		
At 3000 rpm	1.8A or more	1.3A or more
At 8000 rpm	4.0A or less	4.0A or less
Charging coil resistance	0.2 ohm $\pm$ 20% @ 20°C (68°F)	
Lighting coil resistance	0.2 ohm $\pm$ 20% @ 20°C (68°F)	
Lighting output	6.2V or more @ 3000 rpm	
	8.0V or less @ 8000 rpm	

Rectifier (kickstart models)

Make	Mitsubishi	Shinden
Model	SR3AM	S3H-12
Capacity	4A	4A

Rectifier (electric start models)

Make	Stanley
Model	DE4504
Capacity	8A

Voltage regulator

Make	Stanley
Model	SU208Y
Type	electronic
No-load voltage	7.5 volts

Battery (electric start models)
    Capacity 6V 8Ah
    Specific gravity 1.280

Electric starter system (13J SA50 ME only)
    Make .... Nippondenso
    Model ADB3A1
    Type .... Constant mesh
    Output power .... 0.1 kw
    Armature winding resistance .... 0.021 ohm $\pm$ 6% @ 20°C (68°F)
    Brush length .... 7 mm (0.28 in)
    Service limit .... 3.5 mm (0.14 in)
    Brush spring pressure .... 750 $\pm$ 70 g (26.5 $\pm$ 2.47 oz)
    Commutator diameter .... 16.5 mm (0.65 in)
    Service limit .... 15.5 mm (0.61 in)
    Mica undercut .... 0.9 – 1.2 mm (0.0351 – 0.0469 in)
    Starter relay make .... Tateishidenki
    Starter relay model G2MW-D-3670
    Starter relay rating .... 50 $\pm$ 20A
    Relay coil resistance .... 20 ohm $\pm$ 10% @ 20°C (68°F)

Turn signal relay
    Make .... Mitsuba
    Model FR-9T12
    Type .... Heat ribbon
    Frequency .... 90 c.p.m.

---

1 Introduction

    This update Chapter covers the UK SA50 M Passola models from 1982 to 1985. The basic kickstart model has the model identity code of 13H and runs from engine/frame number 2T4-260101 onwards. The SA50 ME electric start version, model identity code 13J runs from engine/frame number 2T4-270101 onwards.

    The 13H kickstart model differs only in detail from the pre-1982 version, and most of the changes are confined to minor specification and tolerance modifications. These alterations will be noted in the accompanying specifications section, and do not affect the working procedures described elsewhere in the Manual.

    The major change on the 13J electric start version is the adoption of the electric starter system, together with a larger capacity battery and an uprated charging system to cope with it. The starter motor is housed behind the transmission cover and drives through a modified 1st speed clutch. Other detail changes include a redesigned oil tank and modified wiring and hose routings. These are shown in Figs. 7.6, 7.7 and 7.8 and discussed where appropriate in the text.

2 Electric starter system: fault diagnosis

    1 In the event of a fault developing in the starter system it is important to attempt diagnosis in a logical sequence. It should be noted that the motor is not particularly easy to reach and so it is worth eliminating any other possible causes first. It is suggested that the checks described below are followed in sequence to avoid unnecessary work.

Starter fails to operate when button is pressed – recurrent fault
2 Is the battery fully charged and in good condition? It must be remembered that the battery is of limited capacity and thus will only be able to crank the engine for a short time before becoming exhausted. Turn the ignition switch on and check that turn signals flash brightly and at the normal rate; if dim or if they

flash only slowly, the battery is too discharged to operate the starter. Examine the battery and top up the electrolyte if necessary (see Routine maintenance, p.10). Start the machine using the kickstart for a day or two to allow the battery to recover, or alternatively recharge the battery **off** the machine at a maximum current of 0.8 amps.
3 If the fault persists or occurs repeatedly, check that the battery has not become faulty due to old age or damage. If the battery is over two years old or so expect to have to renew it. If necessary, a Yamaha dealer can test the battery for you and advise on the best course of action. As a rough guide, if sludge can be seen lying at the bottom of the battery casing it is likely that renewal will be inevitable.
4 Where the battery seems to be in good order but is often too flat to start the engine, check the charging system output as described in Chapter 6 Section 2. Note that the output figures for electric start models are as follows:

Charging system output test – electric start UK models
    Lights off   *1.8A or more at 3000 rpm*
                      4.0A or less at 8000 rpm
    Lights on   *1.3A or more at 3000 rpm*
                     4.0A or less at 8000 rpm

5 Where the charging system output is outside the limits given above, check the charging coil resistance (white lead to black lead) and the lighting coil resistance (yellow lead to black lead). If the readings obtained differ markedly from those shown in the Specifications, it is likely that the relevant coil is damaged. Have the fault confirmed by a Yamaha dealer.

Starter fails to operate when button is pressed – isolated fault
6 If the starting problem has only occurred once, it may be an isolated fault, perhaps due to the battery becoming discharged over a period. This can sometimes happen if the machine is used only for occasional short journeys where it does not have time to recover from the heavy discharge associated with starting. Try taking the machine on a longer run after checking the electrolyte level, or alternatively recharge the battery **off** the machine at a maximum current of 0.8 amps.
7 If the battery is fully charged, check that the starter relay is working. The relay is held in a rubber mounting behind the right-hand side panel, just forward of the ignition coil (see Fig. 7.1). With the panel removed, listen to the relay as the starter button is pressed (ignition switch on). There should be an audible click

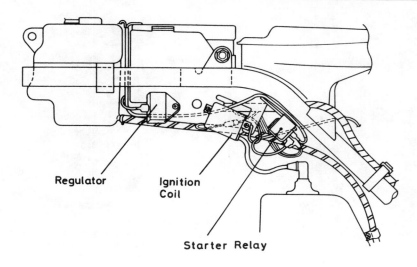

Regulator   Ignition
                   Coil

Starter Relay

Fig. 7.1 Starter relay location

as the relay contacts close. If not, check that the various terminals are attached and secure.

8   If this fails to resolve the fault, the relay may be damaged. Temporarily disconnect the thick battery and motor leads at the relay terminals, leaving the two-wire block connector attached. Connect a multimeter to the battery and motor terminals at the relay, and set it to its resistance (ohms) scale. Switch on the ignition and check that the meter shows zero ohms when the starter button is pressed. If not, pull off the block connector and check the resistance of the relay windings. These should show a reading of about 20 ohms. If zero or infinite resistance is shown, the windings are shorted or open circuit and the relay must be renewed.

9   If the battery is in good order and the relay is working correctly, the fault must lie in the heavy duty lead from the battery to the relay, the motor lead from the relay to the motor, the earth lead between the frame and the transmission casing or in the motor itself. The first three can be checked visually, but if the fault lies in the motor, refer to Section 3 for further information.

3   Electric starter motor: removal and refitting

1   Place the machine on its centre stand, place a drain tray below the transmission casing drain plug, remove the plug and allow the oil to drain. Note that before the cover is removed a new gasket should be on hand in case of breakage. While the oil is draining, remove the front cowl, the side panels and the rear cowl and luggage rack. When removing the latter, note that to gain access to the front left-hand mounting nut it is first necessary to remove the helmet lock assembly. This is held by a single screw which can be reached after the lock has been opened. It is tight and an impact driver will probably be needed. The remaining panels can be removed as described in Chapter 1 Section 3.

2   Disconnect the starter motor lead at the relay terminal and feed it through to the left-hand side of the machine. Remove the transmission cover screws, then carefully lift the cover away. The cover may be a little reluctant to move, so try rocking it to ease it away. If care is taken, the gasket will be undamaged and may be reused. To gain access to the motor, release the three screws which hold the cover plate to the transmission cover. Lift away the cover, then carefully peel off the gasket. The motor is held by two cross-head screws to the inside of the cover.

3   When refitting the motor, carefully clean the rubber seal which blanks off the motor compartment, and ensure that it locates correctly during fitting. Offer up the motor and tighten the mounting screws securely. Fit the transmission cover gasket, then fit the motor cover plate. When refitting the assembled transmission cover, check that the washer is in place on the end of the 2nd speed clutch. Offer up the cover, ensuring that the locating dowels engage. It may help to move the kickstart lever to assist in aligning the starter components. If the cover sticks, do not force it; pull it away and try again.

4   Fit some of the cover screws and check that the kickstart mechanism operates normally before moving on. Do not forget to refit the earth lead which is held by one of the casing screws; this provides the earth connection for the starter motor. Fit the remaining screws and the transmission drain plug, then top up the casing using 650 cc (1.14 Imp pint) of SAE 10W30 Type SE motor oil. Route the starter motor lead back round to the relay and reconnect it. Check that the two-wire block connector is refitted. At this stage, switch on the ignition and check that the starter motor operates normally. If all is well, refit the bodywork and rack.

3.2a Remove the three screws and lift away the cover plate and the gasket

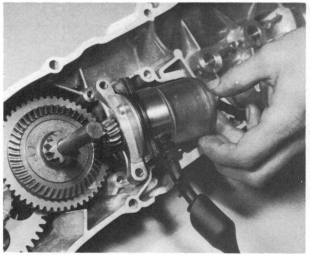

3.2b Remove the two motor retaining screws and lift the motor out of the cover recess

3.3 When refitting the motor check that wiring and motor compartment seals locate correctly

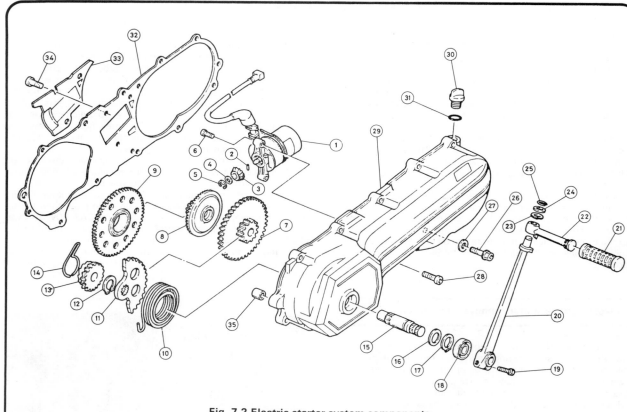

Fig. 7.2 Electric starter system components

1 Starter motor	13 Ratchet gear	25 Circlip
2 Driving pin	14 Friction clip	26 Oil level plug
3 Pinion	15 Kickstart shaft	27 Sealing washer
4 Washer	16 Washer	28 Screw
5 E-clip	17 Circlip	29 Transmission cover
6 Screw – 2 off	18 Oil seal	30 Oil filler plug
7 Kickstart idler gear	19 Pinch bolt	31 O-ring
8 Starter idler gear	20 Kickstart lever	32 Gasket
9 Starter drive gear	21 Lever rubber	33 Cover plate
10 Return spring	22 Lever knuckle	34 Screw – 3 off
11 Kickstart quadrant	23 Spring washer	35 Locating dowel
12 Circlip	24 Washer	

4 Electric starter motor: dismantling, overhaul and re-assembly

1   If a fault in the starter motor is suspected it should be removed for inspection and overhaul as detailed in the preceding Section. Slacken and remove the two screws which retain the motor casing to the cast alloy end bracket and lift the casing away. The motor armature will remain in position in the end bracket and need not be removed unless the commutator or brushes require attention.

2   Examine the copper commutator segments for signs of wear, scoring or discolouration. If the commutator or brushes require further attention, prise off the E-clip which retains the starter motor pinion to the shaft end. Remove the pinion and displace the small driving pin from the shaft. The armature can now be withdrawn from the end bracket.

3   When new, each brush is 7 mm (0.28 in) in length. Measure the brush lengths, renewing them if either is worn down to 3.5 mm (0.14 in) or less. It is easier to accomplish this if the brush holder is released from the end bracket. Remove the cable grommet from the end bracket, then remove the two cross-head screws which retain the brush holder.

4   Before the motor is reassembled, check that the copper commutator segments are clean. The surface can be burnished using fine glass paper. Note that emery cloth or 'wet-and-dry' abrasive paper should not be used; the abrasive particles tend to become embedded in the soft copper segments and will cause rapid brush wear. Remove as little of the commutator material as is necessary to restore it to a clean, smooth surface.

5   If the commutator is badly scored or worn, it may be possible to have it skimmed in a lathe to restore it. This can only be done if there is enough material remaining; if the commutator diameter is reduced to 15.5 mm (0.61 in) or less it will be beyond the wear limit and the motor will have to be renewed. Between each segment is a mica insulator which must be undercut to 0.9 – 1.2 mm (0.0351 – 0.0469 in). If the commutator has been reclaimed by skimming, the mica must be recut. This should be done very carefully using an old hacksaw blade ground to the exact width of the mica insulator. If the skimming was carried out by a vehicle electrical specialist the re-cutting should be carried out as a matter of course.

6   Before the armature is installed, wipe the commutator surface with methylated spirit to remove any grease or dirt. If the condition of the armature is suspect, it can be checked using a multimeter set on the resistance scale. The resistance between any pair of commutator segments should be about 20 ohms. If infinite resistance is shown, it is likely that the windings have broken internally, whilst zero or very low resistance indicate a short circuit in the windings. To check the armature insulation, measure the resistance between the armature core and each segment. If anything other than infinite resistance is shown, the armature insulation must be faulty. If any of the above faults is noted, it will be necessary to fit a new motor – it is not possible to purchase the armature separately. Note that the encapsulated construction of the armature windings makes rewinding virtually impossible.

7   To fit the armature through the brushes it will be necessary to push the latter back into the holders. This is a fiddly job requiring a good deal of patience and if possible, three hands. We found the best approach was to place the armature partly in position and then work the brushes back into their holders using small electrical screwdrivers (see photograph). Once the commutator is in position be very careful not to push it out again; it is advisable to refit the driving pin, pinion and E-clip at this stage to prevent this. Refit the motor casing, tightening the two screws firmly. Check that the grommet and motor compartment seals are correctly located before the motor is refitted.

4.1 Remove the motor end cover leaving the armature in place through the end bracket

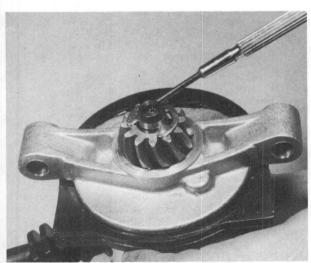

4.2a Pinion is retained on the armature end by an E-clip

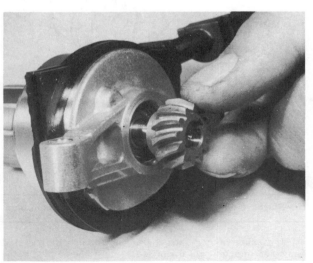

4.2b Slide the pinion off the shaft ...

4.2c ... and displace the driving pin to free armature

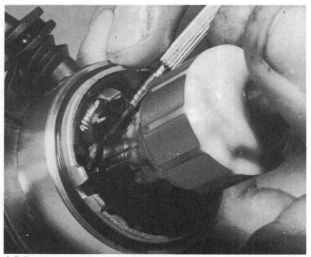

4.7 Brushes may be pushed back into holders to allow the commutator to be slid into place

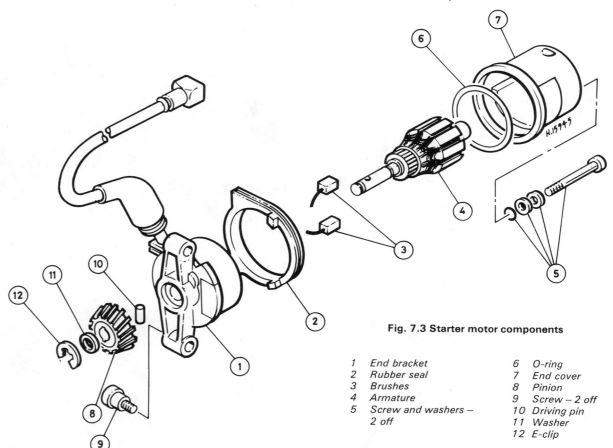

Fig. 7.3 Starter motor components

1	End bracket	6	O-ring
2	Rubber seal	7	End cover
3	Brushes	8	Pinion
4	Armature	9	Screw – 2 off
5	Screw and washers – 2 off	10	Driving pin
		11	Washer
		12	E-clip

5 Starter clutch: dismantling, overhaul and reassembly

1   The starter motor turns the engine through the kickstart gears and through a roller clutch assembly incorporated in the 1st speed clutch unit. To gain access to it, remove the transmission cover as described in Section 3 above. To remove the clutch it will be necessary to prevent the crankshaft from turning. This can be achieved by holding the generator rotor, so before going further, remove the fan cowl which is held by a single screw after the right-hand side panel has been released. Remove the fan securing screws and lift the fan away.

2   Make up a holding tool as shown in the accompanying illustration using steel strip drilled to take the locating bolts. Note that the example shown was designed to fit a variety of engines; a simpler version consisting of a single strip with holes spaced to match the rotor slots will suffice. Fit the bolts so that

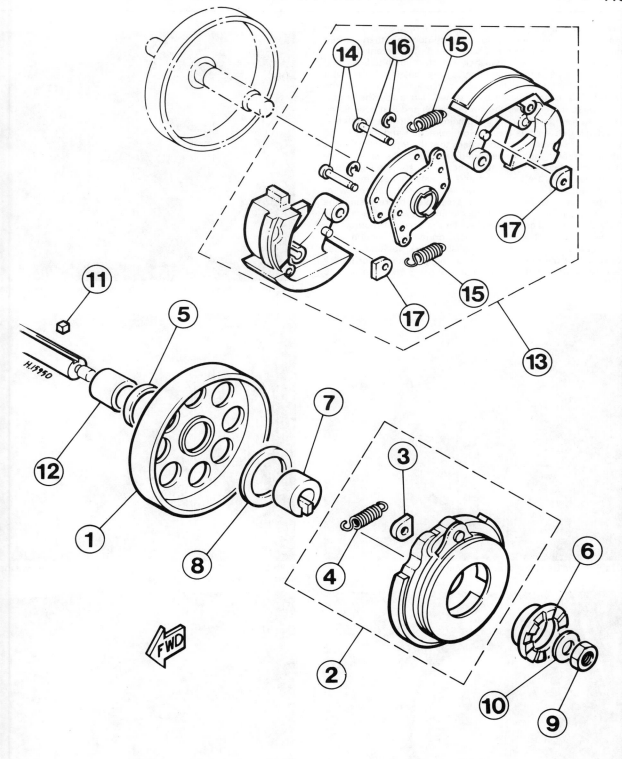

Fig. 7.4 Starter clutch components

1	Clutch hub	7	Keyed boss	13	2nd speed clutch assembly
2	1st speed clutch/starter clutch	8	Thrust washer	14	Retaining pin
3	Damping block	9	Nut	15	Spring – 2 off
4	Spring	10	Belville washer	16	E-clip
5	Ring	11	Woodruff key	17	Damping block
6	Ratchet boss	12	Spacer		

they protrude just enough to engage in the rotor slots. Hold the rotor as shown in the accompanying photograph, then slacken and remove the nut on the left-hand end of the crankshaft.

3   Remove the Belville washer, kickstart ratchet boss and thrust washer, and the caged needle roller bearing. Note that a short Woodruff key section will probably drop clear of the crankshaft slot and should be retained. Lift away the starter driven gear, then remove the starter clutch and first gear clutch assembly. Temporarily refit the driven gear into the clutch hub and check that it spins freely in one direction and locks in the other. If its operation is erratic, check that the three rollers in the hub are smooth and undamaged, and that the springs are unbroken and correctly located. The rollers and the boss upon which they bear are hardened and unlikely to wear in normal use. If damaged in any way, however, they must be renewed.

4   The clutch components are assembled by reversing the removal sequence. Note that the clutch boss will engage more easily if it is turned as it is installed. Fit the smaller Woodruff key in the same slot as the clutch drum key section (see photographs). Fit the Belville washer with its convex face outwards. Fit the retaining nut, hold the generator rotor to lock the crankshaft, and tighten the nut to 2.5 – 3.5 kgf m (18 – 25 lbf ft).

5.2 Home-made holding tool can be used to lock the crankshaft

5.3a Remove Belville washer from centre of ratchet boss

5.3b Lift away the ratchet boss together with the thrust washer which is fitted behind its flange

5.3c The caged needle roller bearing can now be lifted away

5.3d Do not lose the short Woodruff key that locates the boss

5.3e Check condition of rollers, springs and boss

5.4a 1st speed clutch hub is located by a keyed boss ...

5.4b ... against which is fitted the ratchet boss Woodruff key

5.4c Fit clutch shoe/starter clutch assembly as shown

5.4d Do not omit ratchet boss thrust washer

5.4e Lock crankshaft and tighten nut to specified torque

5.4f Before fitting cover, place washer on end of 2nd speed clutch shaft

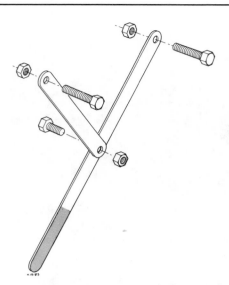

Fig. 7.5 Construction of generator rotor holding tool

6 Cable and wiring routing and component location

1   The adoption of electric starting on the 13J model and the various detail changes has necessitated slight changes to the routing of the various pipes and the electrical wiring. In addition, the machines with starter motors have a larger battery, and this has meant that the oil tank shape has been revised and that the location of some of the electrical components has been altered. The line drawings which accompany this Section illustrate the more significant alterations.

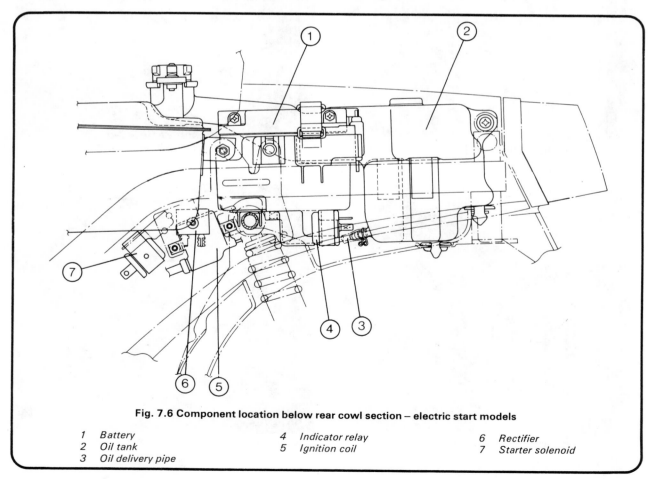

Fig. 7.6 Component location below rear cowl section – electric start models

1	Battery	4	Indicator relay	6	Rectifier
2	Oil tank	5	Ignition coil	7	Starter solenoid
3	Oil delivery pipe				

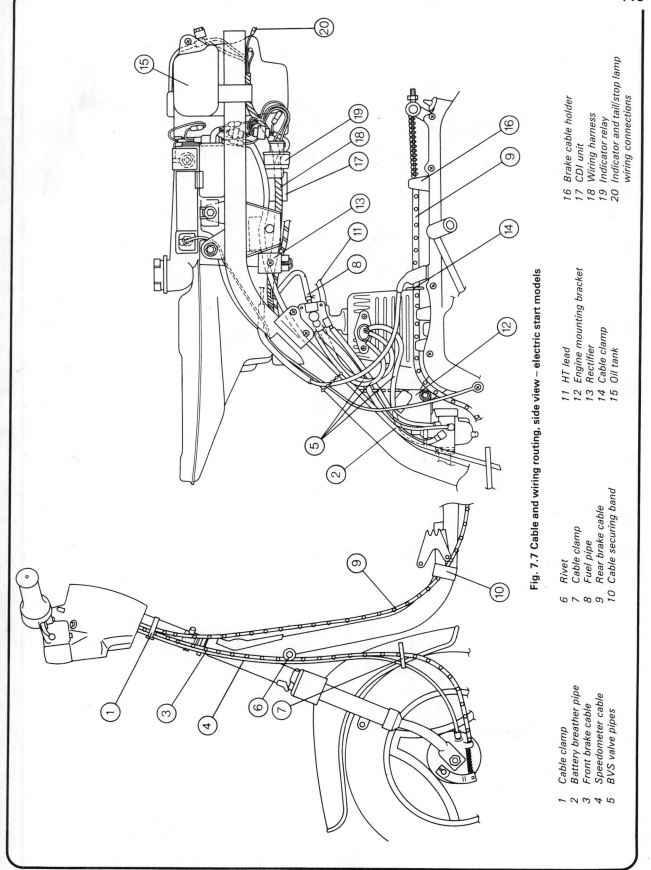

Fig. 7.7 Cable and wiring routing, side view – electric start models

1 Cable clamp
2 Battery breather pipe
3 Front brake cable
4 Speedometer cable
5 BVS valve pipes

6 Rivet
7 Cable clamp
8 Fuel pipe
9 Rear brake cable
10 Cable securing band

11 HT lead
12 Engine mounting bracket
13 Rectifier
14 Cable clamp
15 Oil tank

16 Brake cable holder
17 CDI unit
18 Wiring harness
19 Indicator relay
20 Indicator and tail/stop lamp
   wiring connections

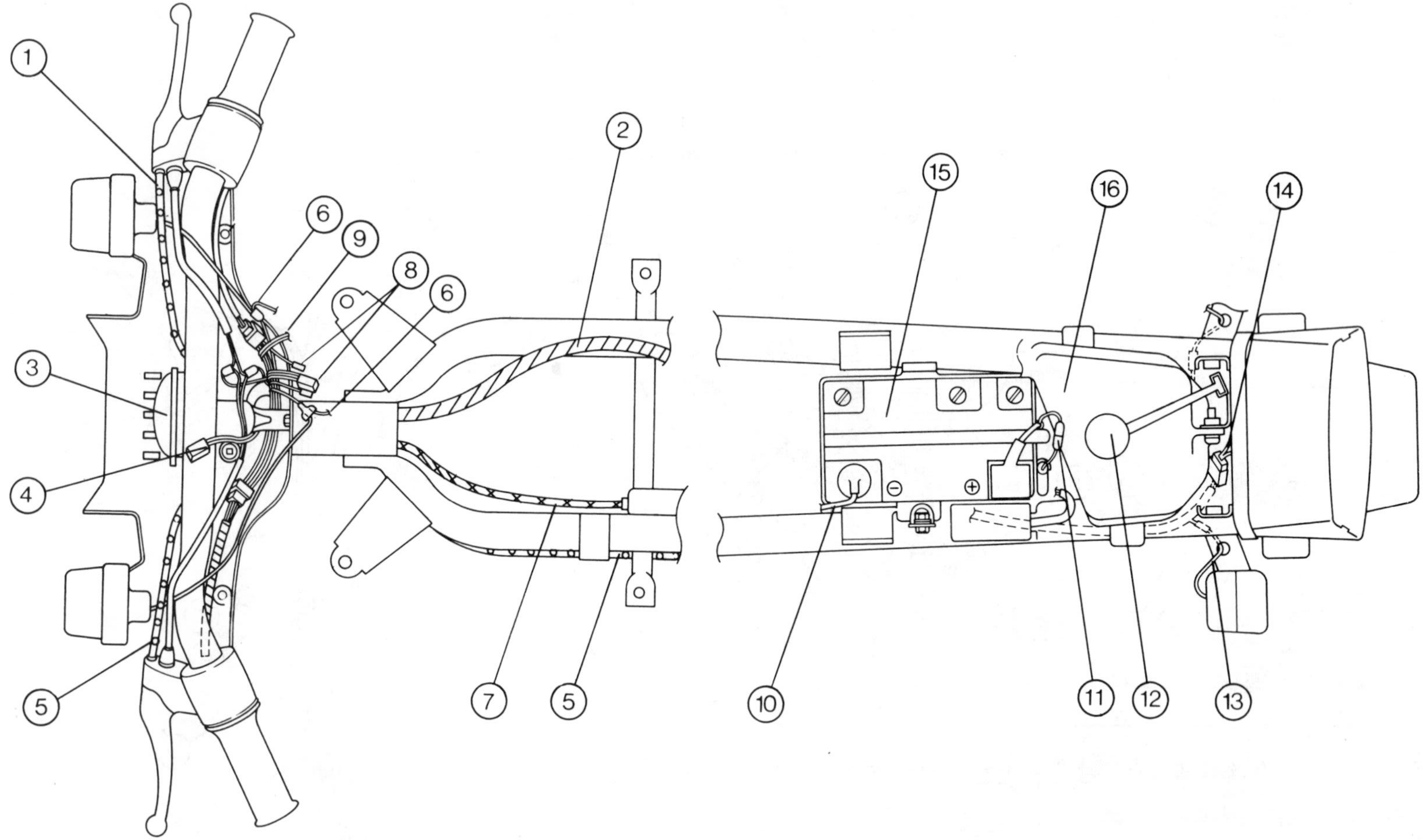

Fig. 7.8 Cable and wiring routing, top view – electric start models

1 Front brake cable
2 Wiring harness
3 Horn
4 Headlamp wiring connector
5 Rear brake cable

6 Indicator warning buzzer wiring connector
7 Throttle cable
8 Ignition switch wiring connector

9 Oil level warning light wiring connector
10 Battery earth terminal
11 Fuse holder
12 Oil level switch

13 Indicator wiring
14 Tail/stop lamp wiring connector
15 Battery
16 Oil tank

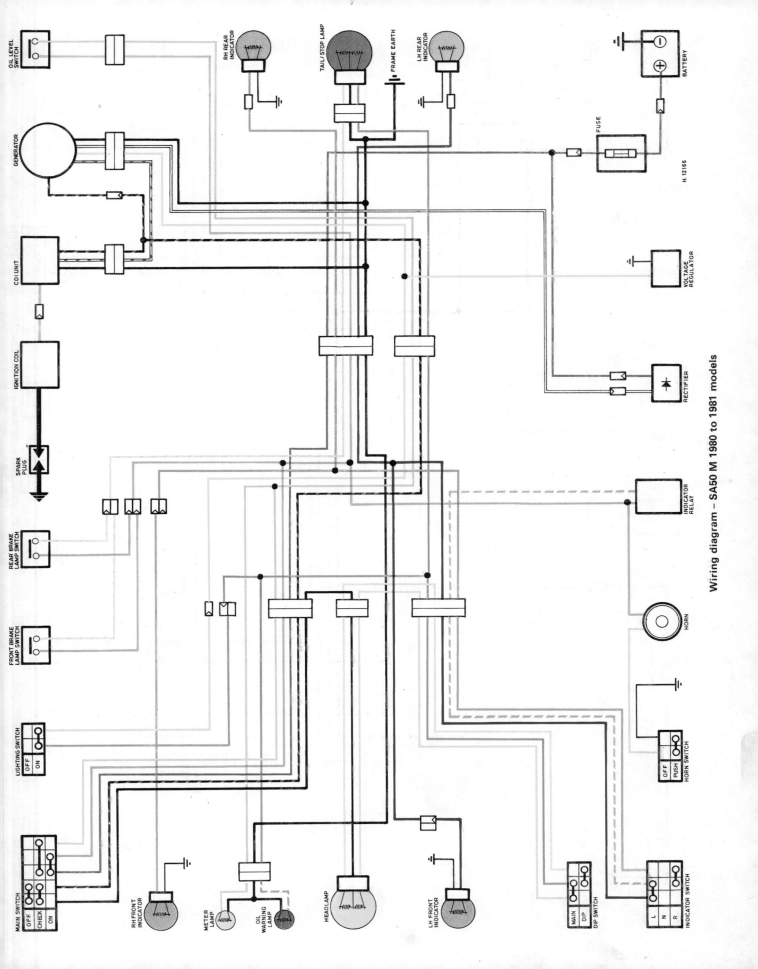

Wiring diagram – SA50 M 1980 to 1981 models

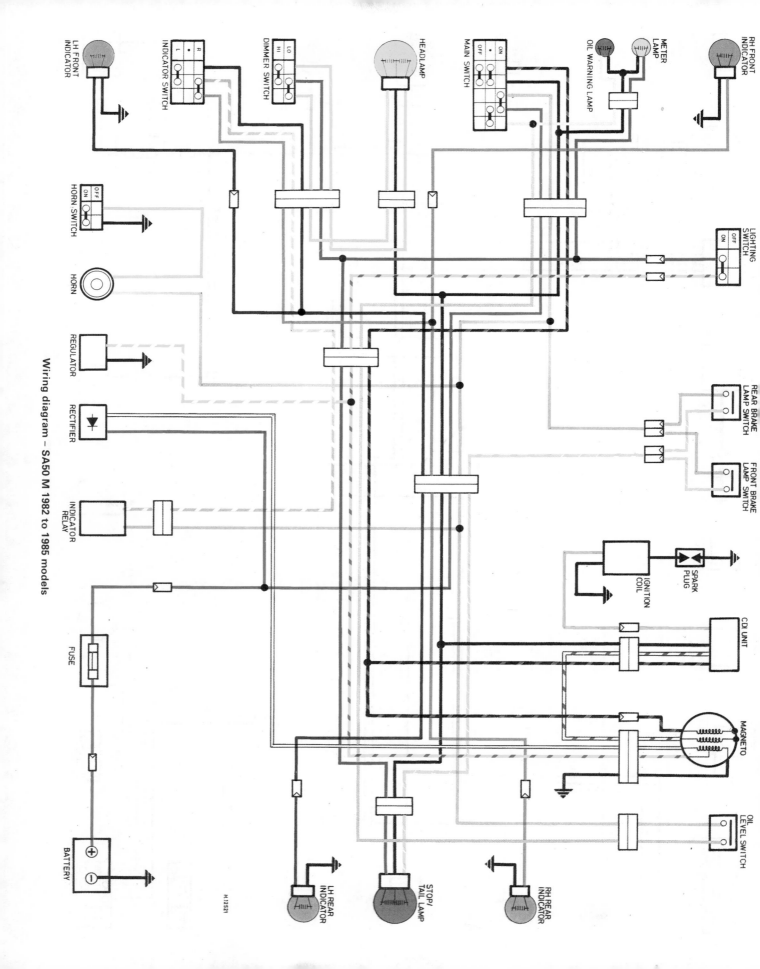

Wiring diagram – SA50 M 1982 to 1985 models

LH FRONT INDICATOR

INDICATOR SWITCH
L · R

DIMMER SWITCH
LO HI

HEADLAMP

MAIN SWITCH
OFF · ON

OIL WARNING LAMP

METER LAMP

RH FRONT INDICATOR

HORN SWITCH
ON OFF

HORN

REGULATOR

RECTIFIER

INDICATOR RELAY

FUSE

BATTERY

LIGHTING SWITCH
ON OFF

REAR BRAKE LAMP SWITCH

FRONT BRAKE LAMP SWITCH

IGNITION COIL

SPARK PLUG

CDI UNIT

MAGNETO

OIL LEVEL SWITCH

LH REAR INDICATOR

STOP/ TAIL LAMP

RH REAR INDICATOR

H.12521

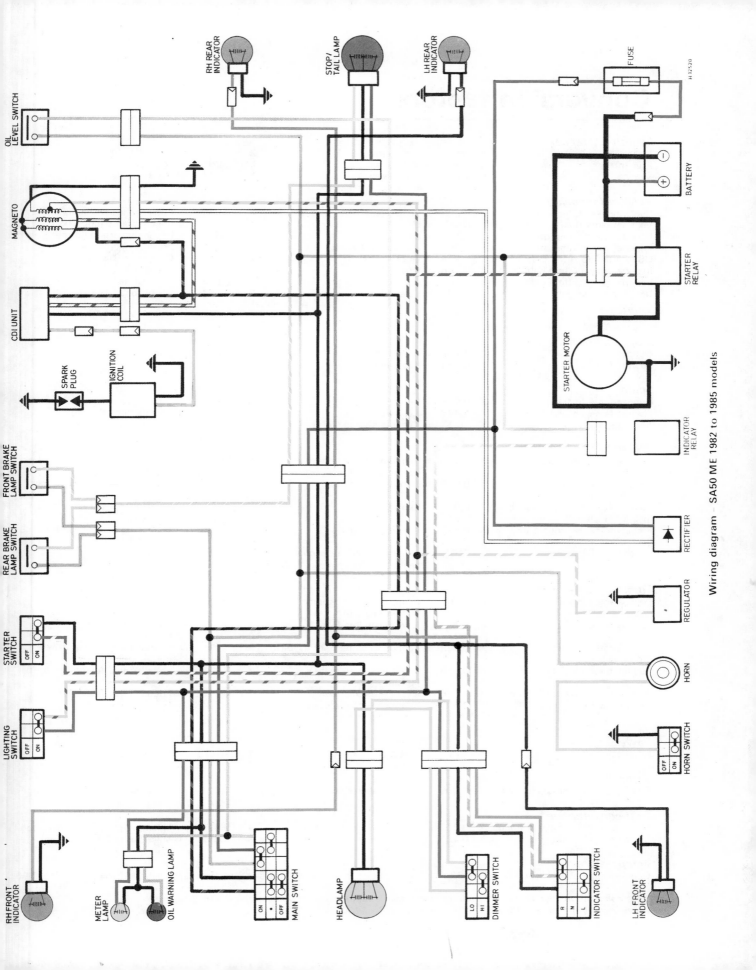

Wiring diagram – SA50 ME 1982 to 1985 models

RH REAR
INDICATOR

STOP/
TAIL LAMP

LH REAR
INDICATOR

FUSE

H.12520

OIL
LEVEL
SWITCH

BATTERY

MAGNETO

STARTER
RELAY

CDI UNIT

STARTER MOTOR

SPARK
PLUG

IGNITION
COIL

INDICATOR
RELAY

FRONT BRAKE
LAMP SWITCH

RECTIFIER

REAR BRAKE
LAMP SWITCH

REGULATOR

STARTER
SWITCH

ON

OFF

HORN

LIGHTING
SWITCH

ON

OFF

HORN SWITCH

ON

OFF

RH FRONT
INDICATOR

METER LAMP

OIL WARNING LAMP

MAIN SWITCH

ON

OFF

HEADLAMP

DIMMER SWITCH

LO   HI

INDICATOR SWITCH

R   N   L

LH FRONT
INDICATOR

Conversion factors

Length (distance)

Inches (in)	X	25.4	= Millimetres (mm)	X 0.0394	= Inches (in)
Feet (ft)	X	0.305	= Metres (m)	X 3.281	= Feet (ft)
Miles	X	1.609	= Kilometres (km)	X 0.621	= Miles

Volume (capacity)

Cubic inches (cu in; in^3)	X	16.387	= Cubic centimetres (cc; cm^3)	X 0.061	= Cubic inches (cu in; in^3)
Imperial pints (Imp pt)	X	0.568	= Litres (l)	X 1.76	= Imperial pints (Imp pt)
Imperial quarts (Imp qt)	X	1.137	= Litres (l)	X 0.88	= Imperial quarts (Imp qt)
Imperial quarts (Imp qt)	X	1.201	= US quarts (US qt)	X 0.833	= Imperial quarts (Imp qt)
US quarts (US qt)	X	0.946	= Litres (l)	X 1.057	= US quarts (US qt)
Imperial gallons (Imp gal)	X	4.546	= Litres (l)	X 0.22	= Imperial gallons (Imp gal)
Imperial gallons (Imp gal)	X	1.201	= US gallons (US gal)	X 0.833	= Imperial gallons (Imp gal)
US gallons (US gal)	X	3.785	= Litres (l)	X 0.264	= US gallons (US gal)

Mass (weight)

Ounces (oz)	X	28.35	= Grams (g)	X 0.035	= Ounces (oz)
Pounds (lb)	X	0.454	= Kilograms (kg)	X 2.205	= Pounds (lb)

Force

Ounces-force (ozf; oz)	X	0.278	= Newtons (N)	X 3.6	= Ounces-force (ozf; oz)
Pounds-force (lbf; lb)	X	4.448	= Newtons (N)	X 0.225	= Pounds-force (lbf; lb)
Newtons (N)	X	0.1	= Kilograms-force (kgf; kg)	X 9.81	= Newtons (N)

Pressure

Pounds-force per square inch (psi; lbf/in^2; lb/in^2)	X	0.070	= Kilograms-force per square centimetre (kgf/cm^2; kg/cm^2)	X 14.223	= Pounds-force per square inch (psi; lbf/in^2; lb/in^2)
Pounds-force per square inch (psi; lbf/in^2; lb/in^2)	X	0.068	= Atmospheres (atm)	X 14.696	= Pounds-force per square inch (psi; lbf/in^2; lb/in^2)
Pounds-force per square inch (psi; lbf/in^2; lb/in^2)	X	0.069	= Bars	X 14.5	= Pounds-force per square inch (psi; lbf/in^2; lb/in^2)
Pounds-force per square inch (psi; lbf/in^2; lb/in^2)	X	6.895	= Kilopascals (kPa)	X 0.145	= Pounds-force per square inch (psi; lbf/in^2; lb/in^2)
Kilopascals (kPa)	X	0.01	= Kilograms-force per square centimetre (kgf/cm^2; kg/cm^2)	X 98.1	= Kilopascals (kPa)

Torque (moment of force)

Pounds-force inches (lbf in; lb in)	X	1.152	= Kilograms-force centimetre (kgf cm; kg cm)	X 0.868	= Pounds-force inches (lbf in; lb in)
Pounds-force inches (lbf in; lb in)	X	0.113	= Newton metres (Nm)	X 8.85	= Pounds-force inches (lbf in; lb in)
Pounds-force inches (lbf in; lb in)	X	0.083	= Pounds-force feet (lbf ft; lb ft)	X 12	= Pounds-force inches (lbf in; lb in)
Pounds-force feet (lbf ft; lb ft)	X	0.138	= Kilograms-force metres (kgf m; kg m)	X 7.233	= Pounds-force feet (lbf ft; lb ft)
Pounds-force feet (lbf ft; lb ft)	X	1.356	= Newton metres (Nm)	X 0.738	= Pounds-force feet (lbf ft; lb ft)
Newton metres (Nm)	X	0.102	= Kilograms-force metres (kgf m; kg m)	X 9.804	= Newton metres (Nm)

Power

Horsepower (hp)	X	745.7	= Watts (W)	X 0.0013	= Horsepower (hp)

Velocity (speed)

Miles per hour (miles/hr; mph)	X	1.609	= Kilometres per hour (km/hr; kph)	X 0.621	= Miles per hour (miles/hr; mph)

Fuel consumption*

Miles per gallon, Imperial (mpg)	X	0.354	= Kilometres per litre (km/l)	X 2.825	= Miles per gallon, Imperial (mpg)
Miles per gallon, US (mpg)	X	0.425	= Kilometres per litre (km/l)	X 2.352	= Miles per gallon, US (mpg)

Temperature

Degrees Fahrenheit = (°C x 1.8) + 32   Degrees Celsius (Degrees Centigrade; °C) = (°F - 32) x 0.56

*It is common practice to convert from miles per gallon (mpg) to litres/100 kilometres (l/100km), where mpg (Imperial) x l/100 km = 282 and mpg (US) x l/100 km = 235

Metric conversion tables

Inches	Decimals	Millimetres	Millimetres to Inches		Inches to Millimetres	
			mm	Inches	Inches	mm
1/64	0.015625	0.3969	0.01	0.00039	0.001	0.0254
1/32	0.03125	0.7937	0.02	0.00079	0.002	0.0508
3/64	0.046875	1.1906	0.03	0.00118	0.003	0.0762
1/16	0.0625	1.5875	0.04	0.00157	0.004	0.1016
5/64	0.078125	1.9844	0.05	0.00197	0.005	0.1270
3/32	0.09375	2.3812	0.06	0.00236	0.006	0.1524
7/64	0.109375	2.7781	0.07	0.00276	0.007	0.1778
1/8	0.125	3.1750	0.08	0.00315	0.008	0.2032
9/64	0.140625	3.5719	0.09	0.00354	0.009	0.2286
5/32	0.15625	3.9687	0.1	0.00394	0.01	0.254
11/64	0.171875	4.3656	0.2	0.00787	0.02	0.508
3/16	0.1875	4.7625	0.3	0.01181	0.03	0.762
13/64	0.203125	5.1594	0.4	0.01575	0.04	1.016
7/32	0.21875	5.5562	0.5	0.01969	0.05	1.270
15/64	0.234375	5.9531	0.6	0.02362	0.06	1.524
1/4	0.25	6.3500	0.7	0.02756	0.07	1.778
17/64	0.265625	6.7469	0.8	0.03150	0.08	2.032
9/32	0.28125	7.1437	0.9	0.03543	0.09	2.286
19/64	0.296875	7.5406	1	0.03937	0.1	2.54
5/16	0.3125	7.9375	2	0.07874	0.2	5.08
21/64	0.328125	8.3344	3	0.11811	0.3	7.62
11/32	0.34375	8.7312	4	0.15748	0.4	10.16
23/64	0.359375	9.1281	5	0.19685	0.5	12.70
3/8	0.375	9.5250	6	0.23622	0.6	15.24
25/64	0.390625	9.9219	7	0.27559	0.7	17.78
13/32	0.40625	10.3187	8	0.31496	0.8	20.32
27/64	0.421875	10.7156	9	0.35433	0.9	22.86
7/16	0.4375	11.1125	10	0.39370	1	25.4
29/64	0.453125	11.5094	11	0.43307	2	50.8
15/32	0.46875	11.9062	12	0.47244	3	76.2
31/64	0.484375	12.3031	13	0.51181	4	101.6
1/2	0.5	12.7000	14	0.55118	5	127.0
33/64	0.515625	13.0969	15	0.59055	6	152.4
17/32	0.53125	13.4937	16	0.62992	7	177.8
35/64	0.546875	13.8906	17	0.66929	8	203.2
9/16	0.5625	14.2875	18	0.70866	9	228.6
37/64	0.578125	14.6844	19	0.74803	10	254.0
19/32	0.59375	15.0812	20	0.78740	11	279.4
39/64	0.609375	15.4781	21	0.82677	12	304.8
5/8	0.625	15.8750	22	0.86614	13	330.2
41/64	0.640625	16.2719	23	0.09551	14	355.6
21/32	0.65625	16.6687	24	0.94488	15	381.0
43/64	0.671875	17.0656	25	0.98425	16	406.4
11/16	0.6875	17.4625	26	1.02362	17	431.8
45/64	0.703125	17.8594	27	1.06299	18	457.2
23/32	0.71875	18.2562	28	1.10236	19	482.6
47/64	0.734375	18.6531	29	1.14173	20	508.0
3/4	0.75	19.0500	30	1.18110	21	533.4
49/64	0.765625	19.4469	31	1.22047	22	558.8
25/32	0.78125	19.8437	32	1.25984	23	584.2
51/64	0.796875	20.2406	33	1.29921	24	609.6
13/16	0.8125	20.6375	34	1.33858	25	635.0
53/64	0.828125	21.0344	35	1.37795	26	660.4
27/32	0.84375	21.4312	36	1.41732	27	685.8
55/64	0.859375	21.8281	37	1.4567	28	711.2
7/8	0.875	22.2250	38	1.4961	29	736.6
57/64	0.890625	22.6219	39	1.5354	30	762.0
29/32	0.90625	23.0187	40	1.5748	31	787.4
59/64	0.921875	23.4156	41	1.6142	32	812.8
15/16	0.9375	23.8125	42	1.6535	33	838.2
61/64	0.953125	24.2094	43	1.6929	34	863.6
31/32	0.96875	24.6062	44	1.7323	35	889.0
63/64	0.984375	25.0031	45	1.7717	36	914.4

Index

Printed by
J H Haynes & Co Ltd
Sparkford Nr Yeovil
Somerset BA22 7JJ England